Beautiful Jesus

UNVEILING BEAUTY IN THE
FEATURES OF THE LORD

DANY GELYANA

Beautiful Jesus

By Dany Gelyana

Beautiful Jesus House

BOOK ORDERS:
www.beautifuljesusministries.com
www.beautifuljesusbook.com

Printed in the United States of America
First edition, first print: March 2018

ISBN-13: 978-0692071779
ISBN-10: 0692071776

DEDICATIONS

To the virgin born perfect Man Who shed His blood and died for me. The resurrected, ascended, glorified, all knowing, ever present and omnipotent King of kings Jesus Christ.

I also dedicate this book to my amazing children Abigail and Nathanael. It is my joy and honor to be your father. My prayer for you both is that you will intimately know our beautiful Lord Jesus. I love you both with all my heart.

INTRODUCTION

It was in prayer that I first began to discover, by revelation of the Holy Spirit, the beautiful Person of Jesus. And each day, I discover there is more to His beauty than I knew the day before.

During personal times of prayer, I find myself enthralled by the various nuances and features of Christ's being. It is in those precious moments of worship and devotion that my spiritual gaze becomes firmly fastened upon the image of the Savior. In those moments, I'm reminded of this truth: everything about Jesus is beautiful. I truly do mean everything. If we rush beyond reflective moments of pause, we can miss the details that inspire a deep appreciation for Who He is. He truly is a wonder to behold.

Looking unto Jesus the author and finisher of our faith; who for the joy that was set before him endured the cross, despising the shame, and is set down at the right hand of the throne of God.
—Hebrews 12:2 (KJV)

We are to look unto Jesus. That is a timeless truth. Throughout the centuries, many have beheld the Lord's beauty, including John, the beloved disciple of Christ. In the first chapter of Revelation, John gives us an awe-inspiring description of Jesus, the Son of God.

And I turned to see the voice that spake with me. And being turned, I saw seven golden candlesticks; And in the midst of the seven candlesticks one like unto the Son of man, clothed with a garment down to the foot, and girt about the paps with a golden girdle. His head and his hairs were white like wool, as white as snow; and his eyes were as a flame of fire; And his feet like unto fine brass, as if they burned in a furnace; and his voice as the sound of many waters. And he had in his right hand seven stars: and out of his mouth went a sharp two-edged sword: and his countenance was as the sun shineth in his strength. And when I saw him, I fell at his feet as dead. And he laid his right hand upon me, saying unto me, Fear not; I am the first and the last.
—Revelation 1:12-17 (KJV)

What John witnessed caused him to fall down like a dead man. The beauty of the Lord was so intense that it was terrifying. Can you imagine that? What beauty can inspire such trembling, such reverence?

Think also of what Daniel wrote about seeing the Lord.

Then I lifted up mine eyes, and looked, and behold a certain man clothed in linen, whose loins were girded with fine gold of Uphaz: His body also was like the beryl, and his face as the appearance of lightning, and his eyes as lamps of fire, and his arms and his feet like in colour to polished brass, and the voice of his words like the voice of a multitude.
—Daniel 10:5-6 (KJV)

Whenever I read such revelations in the Scripture, it stirs within my heart a desire to better know Jesus and to see His features more clearly.

I hunger for the Lord. It is that passion for His beautiful being that has inspired me to write this book. It is an extension of my personal love and adoration for every beautiful detail of His every feature. He's my obsession.

In this book, we will explore how the Scriptures describe Beautiful Jesus. We will reverently and methodically examine, appreciate, and adore the beauty of the Lord, part by part, feature by feature. What so many miss in haste, we will discover in patient meditation. It is my prayer that as you read this book you will see Jesus. I pray that the Holy Spirit would give to you personal, powerful, supernatural, face-to-face encounters with Christ Himself.

We must look at Him, observe Him, and adore Him. Let us gaze upon the features of Jesus. In Him, you will find the answer to your every need, the purpose for your every moment of existence, and the fulfillment of your heart's desire. He is truly the all-in-all, and the Scriptures describe Him as such:

I am Alpha and Omega, the beginning and the end, the first and the last.
—Revelation 22:13 (KJV)

Let us now look to Jesus with purposeful adoration.

CHAPTER 1:1

THE ACT OF PURPOSEFUL ADORATION

Every chapter in this book has been written with the intent of leading you into a place of deep meditation and prayer. I want you to get lost in the beauty of Jesus. So it is very important that I emphasize to you this revelation, this life-changing truth, concerning "purposeful adoration" with which the Lord has entrusted me. "Purposeful adoration" isn't just a term the Lord gave to me; it is a Spirit-led way to pray, to worship, and even to receive from God.

Purposeful adoration is a combination of praise, honor, worship, adoration, and thanksgiving directed toward the physical features of our Lord Jesus Christ. For example, when you, with the eyes of your heart, look at the Lord's beautiful hand, you worship His hand because it's perfect and holy. In addition to worshiping the Lord's hand for its worthiness, you also praise His hand for what it can do. Purposeful adoration is the worship and adoration of the Lord's features, and the praise for the abilities those beautiful features possess. It is taking your time to boast about His features. It is praising each supernatural maneuver they perform.

Depending on where you direct your worship, honor, and praise, you will receive certain blessings and miracles. For example, there is healing in His hand, direction in His back, peace in His forehead, etc.

Purposeful adoration, that blessed form of prayer, is foundational to this book. It is the core revelation of everything I have written to you. But this revelation didn't come to me all at once. The Lord has been revealing bits and pieces of it to me all throughout my life. Only recently have those pieces come together to form a very clear picture.

In the summer of 2015, I began to develop a strong, Holy Spirit-given desire to write a book. After months of sensing a supernatural pull in my heart, I decided to sit in front of my computer and see what was behind this God-given urge. With all my heart, I wanted to write a book—but I didn't want to write just any book. I wanted whatever was written to come from a deep place of fellowship with God.

Of course, my priority is the preaching of the Gospel of salvation through Jesus Christ. However, I knew the Lord would also give me a message for the Church, a message that would distinguish the voice of this ministry.

I always knew God would begin something great in my life through a book, but to be honest with you, I had no idea what to write or even a general idea of what the contents of the book would be. I just knew God was birthing a desire within me, a desire that He would later fulfill with a revelation.

I wanted to hear from God. I wanted to contribute to the wealth of revelation given to the Church over the centuries. Looking back, I now see it was the Lord Who placed that desire within me—but at the same time, made me wait until He revealed the message to me.

God certainly has His ways of processing us. I think He likes making us feel the "fire" in our bones.

So there I sat with a blank mind, staring at a blank computer screen. I sat there, and to my disappointment, nothing at all came to me. In my own efforts, I tried to think of something—anything to write on that blank digital document. I began to type out different titles the book might potentially be called. Nothing made sense.

Then, with a heart filled with faith, I prayed, "Lord, You have given me this desire to write a book, but I have no clue what it is. Let this book come from You."

Suddenly, at that moment, a phrase came to me.

Beautiful Jesus.

I typed it, and the words appeared on my screen. That was it. Nothing immediately followed. No ideas. No flow of creativity. All that came to me in that moment was that title, Beautiful Jesus. Full disclosure: At the time, I didn't really think anything about those words. Still, I saved the document.

About a year later, in the summer of 2016, I was on a lengthy ministry trip, traveling up and down the California coast, stopping in different cities to preach the Gospel.

During this time, I was going through very difficult circumstances. I felt like I was at a crossroad where I had to make some major decisions about my life and ministry. So that short season of travel was like a spiritual retreat for me. I was taking extra time to be alone with the Lord and seek His will for my life. I had completely forgotten about the two words in the document I'd saved.

During one of my stops, I stayed with my parents for a couple of days. They had gone out for a few hours, and I had the house all to myself. Seeking the Lord, somewhat frustrated, I sat down at the dining room table and opened my computer. I randomly came across a forgotten document, and there it was: "Beautiful Jesus."

The page still had only those two words on it.

I looked at that screen. But this time, my mind was not blank. My creativity was not stagnant. At that moment, it was as if a veil had been removed from my eyes, like a curtain had been pulled back to reveal some masterpiece that until then had been in progress. I saw words flashing across my mind that would become chapters: "His beautiful hands," "His beautiful feet," "His beautiful eyes," and so forth.

In that moment, God reminded me of all the times in my life when Jesus had appeared to me and revealed a certain portion of His image. Each encounter with the Lord had highlighted a certain feature: When I was five years old, I saw the Lord's hands.

I was fifteen years old the first time I saw His beautiful countenance. In my early twenties, His beautiful feet were shown to me. All my life, God had been revealing parts of His Son to me.

Until that moment, all those revelations and experiences had seemed random. But they came into perfect alignment as I stared at my computer screen: This was what the Lord had been preparing me for. This was the message I was to deliver to the Church—the purposeful adoration of Beautiful Jesus. This was going to be more than a book; this was my life's message.

Eventually the Lord moved me to begin writing again. Purposeful adoration isn't just a concept to me. It is a revelation and a way of spiritual living. Looking back, I'm amazed I didn't see it sooner.

And so I emphasize to you, "Look at Beautiful Jesus!"

Looking unto Jesus the author and finisher of our faith; who for the joy that was set before him endured the cross, despising the shame, and is set down at the right hand of the throne of God.
—Hebrews 12:2 (KJV)

I used that scripture in my introduction, but you'll see it again throughout this book because there's so much in it. As I looked at that verse, the words "looking unto Jesus" almost floated off the page toward me. The Lord asked, "Son, do you want me to teach you what this means?" I enthusiastically replied, "Yes, Lord, I want to know what it means." Obviously, we'd all say that in response to such a question from the Lord.

Then the Lord spoke. "Look unto Jesus," He said. "Look closely at Him, the Author and the Finisher of your faith. Everything you already need is encapsulated in Him. Look at His hands. Look at His feet. Look at His eyes, and worship Him.

"I have been teaching you this message your entire life."

FOCUSING UPON HIS FEATURES

To this day, I am still progressing in my understanding of what the Lord spoke to me then. There is great depth to this revelation.

When you focus on His beautiful hands, as you worship God and thank Him for the hands of His Son, you begin to receive the benefits of His beautiful touch. When you worship His beautiful eyes, you begin to see as He sees. When you worship His beautiful feet, you begin to receive the benefits for which His feet were pierced. Feature by feature, moment by moment, through purposeful adoration, we receive from Him and become like Him.

You might say I have become somewhat obsessed with the purposeful adoration of Christ. Some might accuse me of being too detailed, too specific. I'll take the charges and the criticisms, so long as I can siphon every bit of knowledge about Jesus that I can. You might say I've taken it too far when I am filled with thankfulness for His rotator cuff of, which enabled Him to stretch forth His arm and touch my life with His hand. I'm thankful for the very bones of Christ, which carried His regal frame from

town to town, as He went about healing the sick and delivering the demon-possessed. I'm thankful for His organs, His nervous system, His hair, His entire being. I am in awe of His lungs, which carry and release the very breath of God.

There is so much to be uncovered in the mystery that is Christ and His beautiful, supernatural body. For though He was entirely God, He dwelt in the flesh. Think about that!

For in Christ lives all the fullness of God in a human body.
—Colossians 2:9 (NLT)

As you read this book, I believe you will begin to appreciate and know His every feature in greater depths. I hope you, too, will become obsessed with every beautiful feature described in the Holy Scripture. Purposeful adoration is easier than you might think.

You see, purposeful adoration, though a term I have coined, is not necessarily a new concept. You may find at times that something specific about the Lord just seems to stand out in your mind—perhaps His healing virtue or His abundant mercy. And that which stands out in your mind inspires you to adore Him. You focus on something you love about Him and become moved to worship. That is purposeful adoration in action.

Now, many practice this sporadically without being aware of it. They may adore something specific about the Lord here and there. And they may even receive the benefits that come from adoring a specific part of His Person.

But very few believers—and I do mean very few—have harnessed the power of focusing intently on something specific about the Lord. And of those who do so regularly, probably only a small percentage of them realize that purposeful adoration is in itself a spiritual practice, an art form.

It is something we must grow in and cultivate. Once you learn the foundation of the prayer language of adoration as a theory, it must become a practice. It will bring something new to your spiritual life on a daily basis. It is quite personal.

Perhaps you are thinking, "This seems too spiritual for me," or "I am not that spiritual."

Let me encourage you with this: Purposeful adoration is not exclusive to the elite among us. It is so simple that anyone can do it. And it is so powerful that I insist it must be practiced by everyone who desires to know the Lord Jesus in a deeper way. Without purposeful adoration, we cannot fulfill the greatest commandment which tells us to love the Lord our God with all we are. We must direct this language of adoration to our Lord Jesus. We have no choice.

Oh, to know every little thing I can find out about Him! I want to love Him with all that I am, just as the Scripture teaches us to do.

Jesus replied, " 'You must love the LORD your God with all your heart, all your soul, and all your mind.' This is the first and greatest commandment."
—Matthew 22:37-38 (NKJV)

We are to love the Lord with all we are—heart, soul, mind, and strength. We are to adore Him with everything. How are we to do this? One of the best ways is to love every part of Him. Leave nothing about Him unworshipped. The more you adore of Jesus, the more He has of you.

Think of the woman who poured the costly perfume upon His body before His burial. She purposefully poured the oil over every inch of His head, His arms, His legs, and His feet. It's essential that we, too, might pour the oil of adoration upon the Lord, missing nothing in our worship.

When Jesus rose from the dead and appeared to His disciples, they touched His hands and feet. That was their natural reaction upon seeing the risen Lord. His disciples, who approached Him on separate occasions, touched His body while worshiping Him.

Thomas, for example, who was at first filled with doubt, was driven to passionate worship upon seeing the Lord.

Eight days later the disciples were together again, and this time Thomas was with them. The doors were locked; but suddenly, as before, Jesus was standing among them. "Peace be with you," he said. Then he said to Thomas, "Put your finger here, and look at my hands. Put your hand into the wound in my side. Don't be faithless any longer. Believe!" "My Lord and my God!" Thomas exclaimed.

Then Jesus told him, "You believe because you have seen me. Blessed are those who believe without seeing me."
—John 20:26-29 (NLT)

When he touched the nail scars of Jesus, Thomas was filled with awe. He already knew the purpose and abilities each of the Lord's features contained. He had seen them in action with his own eyes. He knew the purpose and ability of the Lord's feet, hands, back and entire body. Thomas walked with the Master for three and a half years. Therefore, when he touched the Lord, it was with purposeful adoration. To Thomas, it wasn't just a matter of touching His body for proof of the resurrection. Each feature of the Lord brought powerful memories to his mind. He wasn't just reading an account of the Lord's resurrection; he was handling Someone very precious to him. Can you imagine what thoughts went through his mind?

"This is actually my Jesus! My Lord. My God. The One I know and love. The One I've seen do the miraculous."

I'm convinced that Thomas worshipped quite intentionally. With purposeful adoration in his heart and tears of amazement in his eyes, Thomas reached out his finger and touched the body of the resurrected Lord. He worshipped. And he knew what he worshipped. He knew why he worshipped. We too must know why we are purposefully adoring Him as we worship. We too must know about every feature of the Son of God's body—a body available to us. We must adore it purposefully and intentionally.

THE GLORIFIED BODY OF THE LORD

There is something unique about worshipping the Lord's body, because there is something unique about His body.

Today, when we touch Jesus by faith, we are not only reaching out to the resurrected Lord but also to the glorified Lord.

When Jesus sat down on the throne of Heaven, He had fully accomplished the work of redemption. The glorified body of Jesus possesses the full nature of God. He is omnipresent, omniscient, and omnipotent. This divine nature allows His glorified body to have contact with millions of human beings simultaneously, while being seated on the throne of Heaven. Every time we purposefully adore the Lord Jesus, we will experience the sensation of having His full attention focused directly on us. What a wonderful truth! Because of His glorified form, Jesus can give attention to every prayerful person who seeks an audience with Him. Jesus's glorified body has the ability to make contact with humanity, both individually and corporately, simultaneously. He can make you feel like you are the only one He is focused on, while doing the same for millions of people all around the world.

While working on this book, I began to share its core concepts with a few close friends and family members. Most of the feedback I received was intriguing. However, one of my friends raised very important questions to the effect of, "Can't it be considered idolatry to worship the features of the Lord's body instead of the Lord Himself? Is it Biblical to worship His features?"

I have to admit I felt challenged. But challenge can be a good thing, especially in matters like these.

After weighing the questions, I felt a spark of inspiration and was led this verse:

For in Christ lives all the fullness of God in a human body.
—Colossians 2:9 (NLT)

The body of Jesus isn't just a regular body. It houses the fullness of God. Every part of Him is divine. The hands and the feet of Jesus are the doors through which we offer our worship. We come to His footstool and grasp His feet to offer worship; we clutch His hands and praise His name. We speak into His ears and move His heart. Our worship, love, adoration, praise, exaltation, and honor are given to Jesus through and by His features. His features are the open doors that receive our worship and release His blessings.

When you worship a feature of the Lord, you aren't just worshipping an object with no life, power, or divinity. When you worship a feature of Jesus, you are, in fact, worshipping an aspect of Him. When you worship His hands, you worship a Healer, a Giver of life, a loving Lord Who provides. When you worship His eyes, you are worshiping a compassionate Master and divine Sovereignty. Every time the Lord is worshiped, adored, or called worthy, it is because of what He does or Who He is.

So when we purposefully adore the features of the Lord, we are not literally worshipping a feature—we are worshipping Him through His features. They are open doors into His being. And they pour out to us power, blessings, wisdom, honor, and strength—all divine. Every feature is an access point to something in His nature.

Thomas knew he was worshipping the Divine. We too must react with the deep adoration for every inch of the Glorified Lord. We too must touch His hands and His feet. We must, for ourselves, make contact with Jesus and adore His every feature—features placed upon a glorified body by the hand of the Father.

YOUR GREAT REWARD

As you appreciate and adore each feature of beautiful Jesus, you'll not just receive Him—which is entirely enough—but you will also receive His marvelous benefits. Not only do we satisfy the Lord through purposeful adoration, He satisfies us, too. He meets all our needs and brings His supernatural life into our realm.

Jesus wants us to call upon Him and use the power of His features. He wants to be approached. I dare say He wants to be approached more than you want to approach Him. He waits for you. He wants to give you Himself, as He did to Abraham.

After these things the word of the LORD came unto Abram in a vision, saying, Fear not, Abram: I am thy shield, and thy exceeding great reward.
—Genesis 15:1 (KJV)

Not only does He want to give you Himself, but He wants to bless you abundantly. He wants to give you all that comes with His being—healing, deliverance, peace, joy, and prosperity. If I may say, He loves it when we use Him. He is not a God of demands but a Lord of supply.

Let His eyes perceive on your behalf. Let His hands act on your behalf. Let Him step, speak, breathe, touch, think, and move on your behalf. Let His every feature touch your life, as you and the Lord delight in one another. He wants to abundantly supply all your needs.

I think it's a mistake to try to avoid God's blessings out of false humility. There are many blessings that are ours to claim when we purposefully adore and specifically acknowledge each feature of the Lord. Purposeful adoration is what the Scripture describes as setting our love upon Him. Look at all the wonderful things that are yours when you set your love upon Him!

Because he hath set his love upon me, therefore will I deliver him: I will set him on high, because he hath known my name. He shall call upon me, and I will answer him: I will be with him in trouble; I will deliver him, and honour him. With long life will I satisfy him, and shew him my salvation.
—Psalm 91:14-16 (KJV)

For those who set their love upon Him, the Lord will:

- *Send deliverance: "will I deliver him …"*
- *Send promotion: "I will set him on high …"*
- *Give access to Himself: "I will answer him …"*
- *Involve Himself: "I will be with him in trouble …"*
- *Give honor: "I will … honour him …"*
- *Give longevity: "With long life will I satisfy him …" and*
- *Give greater revelation of Jesus: "… shew him my salvation …"*

Setting our love upon the Lord, purposefully adoring Him, will bless both you and the Lord. It is a reciprocal way of praying. You don't need to go on forever, listing your requests. You just need to worship Him, and everything you need is bound to be found in His features.

Not only is purposeful adoration the act of setting our love upon Jesus through worship, honor, praise, and exaltation, it is also the act of diligently seeking Him.

But without faith it is impossible to please him: for he that cometh to God must believe that he is, and that he is a rewarder of them that diligently seek him.
—Hebrews 11:6 (KJV)

Purposeful adoration is pleasing to God because it is grounded in faith. This diligent seeking brings divine rewards. Therefore, persistent, purposeful adoration invites the rewarding power of God into our lives. Jesus is a rewarder of the people who live their lives in the posture of purposeful adoration. And what, beside the many benefits I listed, can we expect? The Lord rewards us with His glorious body and all that it can do for us. He rewards us primarily with Himself. He said to Abraham, "I am thy shield, and thy exceeding great reward ..." (Genesis 15:1, ASV) So when we purposefully adore Him, He rewards us with Himself. And in Himself, in His physical body, is found all we will ever need or want.

When we practice the purposeful adoration of Beautiful Jesus, we are in effect "diligently seeking" the Lord. We meticulously explore Him. God wants us to become obsessed with the image of Jesus.

And you can set your love upon Him now.

He is beckoning you now to a deeper, more fulfilling relationship with Him. You don't have to wait until Heaven to worship before the Lord. You can do it now by putting His beauty in your mind. May you be lost in the beauty of Jesus as you read each chapter, each truth, of this book.

PURPOSEFUL ADORATION

Lord, as I embark on this new journey after You, help me to meditate upon Your beauty. Help me to see, with clarity, all that You are and all that You so graciously offer me. Thank You for Your every feature. I declare by faith that I am about to see You like I've never seen You before. Amen.

CHAPTER 1:2

THE FIVE INGREDIENTS OF PURPOSEFUL ADORATION

"Purposeful adoration" is a term I have coined to describe a prayerful approach to worship using the following five keys:

• Praise;
• honor;
• worship;
• adoration; and
• thanksgiving.

These five "ingredients" are all used to create a flow in prayer that will bring you to oneness with Christ. And, while the term "purposeful adoration" might not itself be found in the Scripture, the principles that have led to its formation are fundamental Biblical truths. They are the cornerstone concepts of approaching God's throne.

But the key to understanding them, as they are threaded together to form the tapestry of true worshipful prayer, is to understand them in their own right. The study of each concept will yield treasure upon treasure of practical truths. For the sake of brevity and to stay on a singular line of reasoning, I will only summarize their meanings as they relate to this thing I am encouraging you to do.

PRAISE

How does praise apply in purposeful adoration? To find the answer, we have to look at the Hebrew word used most frequently in the Old Testament for "praise." The word hallal appears eighty-eight times. It means "to produce a clear sound" or "to boast, to celebrate, to rave about, to glory in."

When you practice purposeful adoration, true praise will burst through your words toward Jesus. Praise is the verbal expression of your admiration of God. It is a spoken compliment or a positive verbal observation. When you focus on the features of the Lord, there will come from you praise that has a clear and distinct sound.

Note that hallal refers to a "clear" sound. When it comes to true praise, there is no confusion about it. It is a note of celebration and boasting in the features of the Lord, and in their purposes and abilities as they relate to you.

As you focus your praise on the features of Beautiful Jesus, boast in the abilities they produce. Celebrate the manifestation of power that proceeds to you from His hands, feet, eyes, and ears. Speak out about what each feature does. Open your mouth and declare the power of each one. Say, "Your hands are healing hands!" Tell Him, "Your eyes are filled with compassion!" Do this regularly. Do this wholeheartedly.

HONOR

Think about this: We have the honor of honoring Him. Whether or not we give Him the honor due to Him, Jesus is already clothed with honor and majesty.

Bless the LORD, O my soul!
O LORD my God, You are very great:
You are clothed with honor and majesty …
—Psalm 104:1 (KJV)

All of Heaven sings songs to honor Him. Even now, all the beings of God's realm are united in the eternal honoring of Jesus.

Then I looked again, and I heard the voices of thousands and millions of angels around the throne and of the living beings and the elders. And they sang in a mighty chorus:

"Worthy is the Lamb who was slaughtered—
  to receive power and riches
and wisdom and strength
  and honor and glory and blessing."
—Revelation 5:11-12 (NLT)

We have the opportunity to honor Jesus in the most personal, specific, unique way. We have closer access to the Son of God than the angels do. Jesus never invited the angels to dwell in Him and commune with Him as we are invited to do through purposeful adoration.

We can move beyond marveling at Him from the outside and experience what it is to honor Him with oneness. When we apply honor—reverence inspired by awe and appreciation—in our purposeful adoration of Beautiful Jesus, we are glorifying His individual features and their abilities.

WORSHIP

Worship is a major cornerstone of purposeful adoration. Worship speaks of worth (worth-ship). Jesus is worthy of our love and adoration because He first loved us.

We love him, because he first loved us.
—1 John 4:19 (KJV)

We love and adore what we worship, and we worship what we love and adore. Our worship of Jesus springs from our fellowship with Him. In our fellowship with Him, we find the value hidden in the details of His features, and we find the eternal worth of His attributes.

Purposeful adoration teaches you to willfully worship His beautiful features, part by part, and to attribute the necessary worth and value found within them. When we draw near to Him in this manner, He draws a thousand times nearer to us (James 4:8). The worship of Jesus and the fellowship of Jesus go hand in hand. You cannot have one without the other!

ADORATION

Yours, O LORD, is the greatness, the power, the glory, the victory, and the majesty. Everything in the heavens and on earth is yours, O LORD, and this is your kingdom. We adore you as the one who is over all things.
—1 Chronicles 29:11 (NLT)

Although the word "adore" only appears in the Scriptures in the verse above, the concept of adoration is still a biblical principle. Adoration is the deep love and appreciation of something. When I adore someone or something, I am giving the subject my attention while focusing on its beauty, while allowing myself to be moved by said beauty.

With a deep love in our hearts, we must practice adoration for the various beautiful features of the Lord. We must be consumed by their beauty.

When visiting the baby Jesus, the Magi fell down and worshipped Him. They so adored the Lord that they were moved to offer gifts. I believe they adored the little baby, the King of the Universe.

And when they were come into the house, they saw the young child with Mary his mother, and fell down, and worshipped him: and when they had opened their treasures, they presented unto him gifts; gold, and frankincense, and myrrh.
—Matthew 2:11 (KJV)

The Book of Revelation is filled with examples of songs of adoration being sung to Jesus in Heaven. Sung from the mouths of angelic beings and glorified saints, they are songs of deep love and respect for Who Jesus is, what His features can do, and their beauty. There is a certain intoxication that comes with adoring the Lord.

THANKSGIVING

In the context of the purposeful adoration of beautiful Jesus, I would define thanksgiving as praise for what Christ's features can accomplish in our lives. We praise and thank Him for His abilities. Whether we are thanking Him by faith in advance for something yet to be received, or for something He has already done on our behalf, we are always right to praise Him for His abilities.

Unto thee, O God, do we give thanks, unto thee do we give thanks: for that thy name is near thy wondrous works declare.
—Psalm 75:1 (KJV)

And giving thanks to the Lord actually allows God to continue to move in our lives.

And he commanded the people to sit down on the ground: and he took the seven loaves, and gave thanks, and brake, and gave to his disciples to set before them; and they did set them before the people.
—Mark 8:6 (KJV)

Jesus gave thanks and broke bread. His hands multiplied food after giving thanks. It is the giving of thanks that multiplies the current blessing. Let thanksgiving pour forth from deep within your spirit. Let it fall upon the beautiful features of our Lord.

Giving thanks always for all things unto God and the Father in the name of our Lord Jesus Christ ...
—Ephesians 5:20 (KJV)

In every thing give thanks: for this is the will of God in Christ Jesus concerning you.
—1 Thessalonians 5:18 (KJV)

By him therefore let us offer the sacrifice of praise to God continually, that is, the fruit of our lips giving thanks to his name.
—Hebrews 13:15 (KJV)

That I may publish with the voice of thanksgiving, and tell of all thy wondrous works.
—Psalm 26:7 (KJV)

CHAPTER 1:3

PURPOSEFUL ADORATION AND MARY

Mary, the blessed mother of Jesus, is also the mother of purposeful adoration. Speaking strictly of the body of the Lord, which must have possessed supernatural power in its own unique way, neither a single person on earth, nor a single angel in Heaven, had the opportunity to adore the body of Jesus as Mary did. Not even God the Father could adore Jesus from her perspective.

Mary was the mother of purposeful adoration, because she worshiped the holy body of Jesus while it still was forming as an embryo within her womb. This makes her the first person to practice purposeful adoration (as it relates to Christ's physical body) or even have contact with the physical body of the Lord. Before Jesus would ever stretch out His hand to touch the sick, His tiny, frail body touched the safety of Mary's womb.

When Mary was pregnant with the precious body of Jesus, she was aware that she was carrying the divine body of the Son of God within her womb. She knew the child was the Son of the Highest, the King of Heaven and Earth. Mary was fully aware that she had been entrusted by God to care for the physical body of His divine Son.

Before Jesus was born, Mary believed and knew the Child in her womb, Who would come into the world through her body, was the holy Son of God:

Mary said to the angel, "How can this be, since I am a virgin?" The angel
answered and said to her, "The Holy Spirit will come upon you, and the
power of the Most High will overshadow you; and for that reason the holy
Child shall be called the Son of God."
—Luke 1:34-35 (NASB)

Mary knew the messianic prophecies. She knew Who Jesus was. Mary
understood the weightiness of the matter. It was made clear to her, by
means of prophetic declaration, that she would carry God within her womb.

And the angel said unto her, Fear not, Mary: for thou hast found favour
with God. And, behold, thou shalt conceive in thy womb, and bring forth a
son, and shalt call his name Jesus. He shall be great, and shall be called
the Son of the Highest: and the Lord God shall give unto him the throne of
his father David.
—Luke 1:30-32 (KJV)

And the presence of the Holy Spirit was so powerful upon Mary that even
those around her were filled with the Spirit and received revelation of
Jesus's identity.

And it came to pass, that, when Elisabeth heard the salutation of Mary, the
babe leaped in her womb; and Elisabeth was filled with the Holy Ghost:
And she spake out with a loud voice, and said, Blessed art thou among
women, and blessed is the fruit of thy womb. And whence is this to me, that
the mother of my Lord should come to me?
—Luke 1:41-43 (KJV)

When the Holy Spirit overshadowed Mary, He not only allowed the eternal Word to supernaturally enter her womb, but He also placed a divine love into Mary that caused her to give birth to the love language of purposeful adoration. The Holy Spirit knows Jesus intimately and loves Him deeply. He knows the power stored in the features of Jesus, because He formed Him in the womb, part by part.

The Holy Spirit is an expert on the features of Jesus and what they disperse, for He is the One Who flows through those features. He is the One Who formed those features. And the Holy Spirit injected His own love for Jesus into Mary's soul at the Conception, making the Holy Spirit the enabler of purposeful adoration and Mary the mother of it. With the first coming of the Lord to the earth, that love language of prayer came into the world by Him and through her.

We see Mary's first recorded expression of purposeful adoration in her response to Elizabeth's prophetic outburst:

And Mary said, My soul doth magnify the Lord, And my spirit hath rejoiced in God my Saviour.
—Luke 1:46-47 (KJV)

Mary's soul began to worship and magnify the "Lord." Mary magnified Jesus, Who was forming in her womb as an embryo, limb by limb, part by part. Think about that! She was the first to start practicing the purposeful adoration of Jesus, as He was forming within her.

We too must magnify the adoration of every divine feature of Jesus and exalt Him purposefully through the Holy Spirit. Let us love those limbs and features as Mary did. Let us practice purposeful adoration in our lives daily.

Furthermore, Mary also knew the cross awaited Jesus (before anyone else did), for she called Jesus her "God" and "Savior" (Luke 1:47).

She believed the Gospel before she was with child. From the moment He was born, the day Jesus would die on the cross was continuously on Mary's mind. Therefore, she relentlessly focused her worship and adoration on the body of the Lord.

Purposeful adoration is to magnify the Lord feature by feature, and worship Him part by part. Mary was worshiping the Lord while His physical parts and features were developing in her womb. She was practicing purposeful adoration in its very beginning stages of development. Mary began to adore and worship the Lord Jesus from the beginning of His formation, through His infancy, through His childhood and adolescent years, and onward into eternity. She knew Who He was and what His mission on earth was. Since the moment Gabriel appeared and announced Jesus to her, Mary believed. I can just see Mary holding Jesus as an infant, rubbing His face with purposeful adoration, fully aware that He was the Lord of Glory.

Mary knew Jesus would suffer and die for the sins of the world. She knew He would rise from the dead and reign forever.

It was prophesied to her from before the time He was born and throughout His childhood. When she kissed His beautiful hands and feet, she knew they would one day be nailed to the cross. Mary purposefully loved Jesus as her personal Lord and as her own child.

Mary knew Jesus would suffer and that she would feel extreme anguish of the soul when that day arrived. She knew and believed His body was God's best sacrifice, the Lamb of God, the divine gift to humanity. Mary often kept the things she witnessed in her heart. This verse, among others, shows us the Gospel she knew and believed:

(Yea, a sword shall pierce through thy own soul also,) that the thoughts of many hearts may be revealed.
—Luke 1:35 (KJV)

Mary, along with the Magi, worshipped Jesus when He was still a young child.

And when they were come into the house, they saw the young child with Mary his mother, and fell down, and worshipped him: and when they had opened their treasures, they presented unto him gifts; gold, and frankincense and myrrh.
—Matthew 2:11 (KJV)

When the wise men "fell down and worshipped" the Child Jesus, I don't believe Mary and Joseph stood by idly. Based on what we have already learned, that Mary was worshipping Jesus even during His embryonic stage, we can conclude that she joined in with the wise men and also worshipped Jesus.

The word translated as "worshipped," in the original language, means to "to kiss the hand (towards) one, in token of reverence." Think about the acclaimed wise men, in humble worship and adoration, kissing the holy hand of a two-year-old Jesus. They were acknowledging that He was their Superior, the eternal King. The wise men offered gifts to Jesus, gifts that revealed His divine nature and mission on earth. The gold spoke about His divinity and kingship. The frankincense spoke to His eternal priestly role. And the myrrh spoke of His sufferings and death at the cross.

Mary and the wise men knew the hand they were bowing down to and kissing was a royal hand. They knew Jesus's little body was holy, destined to suffer for the sins of the world. It was no secret to Mary that her baby and Savior Jesus would one day suffer greatly for us all. This was the beauty of her purposeful adoration. She worshipped Him part by part, knowing the cross was waiting. So we can never take the cross out of our purposeful adoration.

Of course, we all know about Jesus's suffering upon the cross, but Mary knew about it before anyone else did. I wonder what unrecorded exchanges took place between Jesus and His earthly mother. They shared many special moments together. As a mother, Mary continually practiced purposeful adoration.

The love of Mary followed Jesus from pregnancy all the way to the cross.

Before breathing His last breath, Jesus said something to John, something that speaks volumes to me.

When Jesus therefore saw his mother, and the disciple standing by, whom he loved, he saith unto his mother, Woman, behold thy son! Then saith he to the disciple, Behold thy mother! And from that hour that disciple took her unto his own home.
—John 19:26-27 (KJV)

When Jesus told John to "behold thy mother" (prompting John to take her into his home), He was speaking a message with broader application to us all. In essence, I believe Jesus was saying, "Take the lifestyle of Mary into your own home and into your own heart." We are called to practice this love language of Jesus by focusing our love and adoration on Him, feature by feature, just like Mary did.

When Jesus said to her "behold thy son," Jesus was implying that a new breed of lovers would be emerging into the earth after He rose from the dead. This new breed would love Jesus in the pattern that Mary initiated by living a lifestyle of the daily purposeful adoration of beautiful Jesus.

So let us, in part, pattern our adoration of Christ like Mary's.

Mary grieved over His suffering.

Think about Mary watching her Son hanging on the cross for six hours. It was her greatest anguish to watch her Son tortured and crucified. Surely she believed the promises of the suffering Christ, but she still sorrowed over them. Yes, Mary knew what awaited her beloved Son, but watching it actually occur was difficult for her to endure. She watched the nailing of His beautiful hands and feet to the cross. She saw His arms tied to that cruel tree. I'm sure witnessing the crucifixion of Jesus was something that kept Mary awake for long nights preceding His resurrection.

Mary watched the features that she loved and cared for being viciously tormented. We must see the features of our glorified Master on the cross in the same manner. Jesus said that when we take communion, we are to do it in remembrance of Him. Remember His features and body on the cross. Remember the suffering and then worship Him through the cross.

Then he took a cup of wine and gave thanks to God for it. Then he said, "Take this and share it among yourselves. For I will not drink wine again until the Kingdom of God has come." He took some bread and gave thanks to God for it. Then he broke it in pieces and gave it to the disciples, saying, "This is my body, which is given for you. Do this to remember me." After supper he took another cup of wine and said, "This cup is the new covenant between God and his people—an agreement confirmed with my blood, which is poured out as a sacrifice for you."
—Luke 22:17-20 (NLT)

CHAPTER 1:4

PURPOSEFUL ADORATION AND KING DAVID

My purpose in writing this book is to acquaint you with this concept, this way of praying: purposeful adoration. And as I present my reasons for why you should include this form of praying in your own devotion toward God, I'll be sharing my heart with you.

But it's not just me. I'm not the only one who prays in a worshipful way which focuses on the various features of the Lord. In fact, there was a prominent Biblical figure who did the same: King David, whom the Bible describes as "a man after (God's) own heart." 1 Samuel 13:14 (NLT)

We too can be people after God's own heart. To become this, I believe it helps to pray as David did.

If you look closely, you'll notice David's whole life was full of purposeful adoration. His prayers and songs—found throughout the Book of Psalms—show David worshiping, singing, and praying about the Lord's features and their abilities. He even prayed through those features to some extent, calling upon God's ability to work in his favor.

David showed us what a heart aflame and filled with purposeful adoration looks like. He saw the coming Messiah and prophetically knew about His glory. David put on display the fulfillment of the greatest desire in God's heart: that people would worship everything about His Son Jesus.

God's heart is all about Jesus. Therefore, when you practice the purposeful adoration of the Son of God, you are pleasing God's heart in fullness. When we choose to live a lifestyle of purposeful adoration, we gain a special place in the heart of God. We become the people who offer sweet incense to the Lord. We gain a favored place of pleasure within His heart and mind. Practicing purposeful adoration makes us people after the heart of God, because He is seeking people who will "worship in Spirit and in truth." John 4:24 (NKJV) Why? Because God takes great pleasure in His Son Jesus.

And a voice from heaven said, "This is my dearly loved Son, who brings me great joy."
—Matthew 3:17 (NLT)

David understood the value of and richness of purposeful adoration. He was a master of it. David prophetically practiced purposeful adoration, even before the appearance of the Lord Jesus, Who would come through David's lineage. David's heart of purposeful adoration so touched God that He ordained Jesus to be mentioned as the son of David just a few generations later (according to the natural line of Mary). In fact, I believe the entire genealogy of Jesus was full of people who practiced purposeful adoration in one way or another. God places a special crown of honor on the heads of the people who practice this love language toward Jesus.

God trusted David with special revelation about His Son's features and their abilities. Throughout the Book of Psalms, David is uncovering the glory and power found in various features of the Lord.

David sang about them and prayed through them. David praised and boasted of those features constantly. David prophetically foretells Jesus's hands and feet being nailed to the cross and the vicious effects of Calvary on His body.

My life is poured out like water,
   and all my bones are out of joint.
My heart is like wax,
   melting within me.
My strength has dried up like sunbaked clay.
   My tongue sticks to the roof of my mouth.
   You have laid me in the dust and left me for dead.
My enemies surround me like a pack of dogs;
   an evil gang closes in on me.
   They have pierced my hands and feet.
I can count all my bones.
   My enemies stare at me and gloat.
They divide my garments among themselves
   and throw dice for my clothing.
—Psalm 22:14-18 (NLT)

Look at all the features mentioned in that portion of Scripture alone! We see the Lord's bones, heart, tongue, hands, and feet.

Why would God reveal so much intimate knowledge to David about the features and the nature of the coming Messiah? It's because purposeful adoration unlocks the secrets in the heart of God and reveals Jesus in fullness. God wants us, above all else, to worship Jesus and love Him purposefully like David, Mary, and the twenty-four elders do.

Below are a few verses from Psalms that show us prayer, worship, declaration, and revelation about and through the features of the Lord.

HIS HANDS

Sing a new song to the LORD, for he has done wonderful deeds. His right hand has won a mighty victory; his holy arm has shown his saving power!
—Psalm 98:1 (NLT)

In his hand are the deep places of the earth: the strength of the hills is his also.
—Psalm 95:4 (KJV)

Though he fall, he shall not be utterly cast down: for the LORD upholdeth him with his hand.
—Psalm 37:24 (KJV)

HIS FEET

He bowed the heavens also, and came down: and darkness was under his feet.
—Psalm 18:9 (KJV)

For dogs have compassed me: the assembly of the wicked have inclosed me: they pierced my hands and my feet.
—Psalm 22:16 (KJV)

HIS EYES

The LORD is in his holy temple, the LORD's throne is in heaven: his eyes behold, his eyelids try, the children of men.
—Psalm 11:4 (KJV)

Behold, the eye of the LORD is upon them that fear him, upon them that hope in his mercy ...
—Psalm 33:18 (KJV)

I will instruct thee and teach thee in the way which thou shalt go: I will guide thee with mine eye.
—Psalm 32:8 (KJV)

The eyes of the LORD are upon the righteous, and his ears are open unto their cry.
—Psalm 34:15 (KJV)

He ruleth by his power for ever; his eyes behold the nations: let not the rebellious exalt themselves. Selah.
—Psalm 66:7 (KJV)

HIS MOUTH

By the word of the LORD were the heavens made; and all the host of them by the breath of his mouth.
—Psalm 33:6 (KJV)

Remember his marvellous works that he hath done; his wonders, and the judgments of his mouth ...
—Psalm 105:5 (KJV)

With my lips have I declared all the judgments of thy mouth.
—Psalm 119:13 (KJV)

The law of thy mouth is better unto me than thousands of gold and silver.
—Psalm 119:72 (KJV)

Quicken me after thy lovingkindness; so shall I keep the testimony of thy mouth.
—Psalm 119:88 (KJV)

HIS EARS

In my distress I called upon the LORD, and cried unto my God: he heard my voice out of his temple, and my cry came before him, even into his ears.
—Psalm 18:6 (KJV)

The eyes of the LORD are upon the righteous, and his ears are open unto their cry.
—Psalm 34:15 (KJV)

Lord, hear my voice: let thine ears be attentive to the voice of my supplications.
—Psalm 130:2 (KJV)

Give ear, O my people, to my law: incline your ears to the words of my mouth.
—*Psalm 78:1 (KJV)*

HIS NOSE

There went up a smoke out of his nostrils, and fire out of his mouth devoured: coals were kindled by it.
—*Psalm 18:8 (KJV)*

Then the channels of waters were seen, and the foundations of the world were discovered at thy rebuke, O LORD, at the blast of the breath of thy nostrils.
—*Psalm 18:15 (KJV)*

ONLY JESUS

It is most certainly safe to say King David understood and appreciated the power of the Lord's features. He focused his worship toward specific attributes of God. Looking to Psalm 115, we gain even further insight into the power of the Lord's features, as the psalmist compares the Lord and powerless, lifeless idols.

Not to us, O Lord, not to us,

> *but to your name goes all the glory*
> *for your unfailing love and faithfulness.*

Why let the nations say,

> *"Where is their God?"*

Our God is in the heavens,

> *and he does as he wishes.*

Their idols are merely things of silver and gold,

> *shaped by human hands.*

They have mouths but cannot speak,

> *and eyes but cannot see.*

They have ears but cannot hear,

> *and noses but cannot smell.*

They have hands but cannot feel,

> *and feet but cannot walk,*
> *and throats but cannot make a sound.*

And those who make idols are just like them,

> *as are all who trust in them.*

—Psalm 115:1-8 (NLT)

The abilities found in the features of the Lord separate Him and exalt Him above anything or anyone else that might compete for our adoration and worship. In what else can you place your trust? Who else is as worthy of your adoration?

Whom have we in Heaven but He? Only Jesus is able. Only in His hands should you place your trust. Only His feet should you follow. Only His voice should you hear. He is the living, breathing Lord. And His abilities are manifested in His active features.

ENTRUSTED

It's wonderful to see how God so entrusted David with special revelation about His Son's features and their abilities. That sort of revelation is given to those who simply adore the Lord, as King David so often did in his poetic psalms of worship and praise.

CHAPTER 1

HIS BEAUTIFUL COUNTENANCE

Since I was young, the Lord has had His gracious hand upon me. I attribute the grace I have received from Him partly to the godly heritage my parents and grandparents imparted to me. Their constant prayers have provided for me a spiritual safeguard. God has been faithful to them, and God has been faithful to me. Their commitment to the Lord has yielded a generational blessing from which I have greatly benefitted.

When I was five years old, beautiful Jesus appeared to me. I saw the Lord. Yes, I mean that He actually appeared to me in a vision. I could see His beautiful hands stretched out toward me. Naturally, I reached out to Him, and as I did, I felt His weighty, invisible power physically come on my hands!

A few years later, when I was sixteen, I began to fellowship with the Holy Spirit. Unfortunately, that special fellowship was disrupted by a season of rebellion. I drifted from that precious place. I began to delve into things I had no business delving into. I began to read books about New Age spirituality, worldly philosophy, and ungodly poetry. I was spiritually adrift for several years, walking in rebellion. I write this so you might be encouraged to know the Lord is gracious enough to offer you another chance.

Though I had forgotten about the Lord, He didn't forget about me. He remembered our time together, and He sought me.

For about six to eight months before I turned twenty-one, I sensed a strong pull from the Lord. He was inviting me to know Him again. He began to soften my heart and call me to Himself. Every few months, He would touch me; I would be able to sense Him around me. The Lord was preparing me for a transformative encounter with Him.

A short time after I turned twenty-one, I received a phone call from an Egyptian pastor who prayed for me over the phone. When I hung up, something wonderful happened: The Lord Jesus walked into my bedroom. Once again, I was able to see Him. His face was so very bright, just as the Bible describes! His very countenance was beaming with what felt like currents of love and power. Divine essence erupted from Him.

The moment He entered my room, His light revealed two demonic figures nearby. But they were gone as quickly as they were revealed; in an instant, they fled! It was as if they dissolved in His light. Beautiful Jesus was so radiant that His very being repelled the demonic powers. They were forced out of the room by the glory of the Son of God. I was immediately liberated—spiritually and mentally.

He was merciful to me.

After this encounter, I went into a three-year period of secluded prayer, a season of consecration. I again began to fellowship with the Lord. I became dedicated to the Word. From the ages of twenty-one to twenty-four, I was locked away with Jesus. My entire life was transformed just by the countenance of the Lord.

… the LORD turn his face toward you and give you peace.
—*Numbers 6:26 (NIV)*

His countenance alone was enough to bring me peace. His countenance brought peace to my mind, peace to my soul, and peace between me and God.

And there is so much to His peace-giving countenance.

The Son is the radiance and only expression of the glory of [our awesome] God [reflecting God's [a]Shekinah glory, the Light-being, the brilliant light of the divine], and the exact representation and perfect imprint of His [Father's] essence, and upholding and maintaining and propelling all things [the entire physical and spiritual universe] by His powerful word [carrying the universe along to its predetermined goal]. When He [Himself and no other] had [by offering Himself on the cross as a sacrifice for sin] accomplished purification from sins and established our freedom from guilt, He sat down [revealing His completed work] at the right hand of the Majesty on high [revealing His Divine authority] …
—*Hebrews 1:3 (AMP)*

Jesus is not a reflection of the light of God; He is Himself that light. Jesus is the radiance of Heaven. From His face shines all the warmth and brilliance of God's goodness and love.

Just as the sun's light brings growth and gives sustenance to plants and vegetation, so the face of Jesus causes the fruit of the Spirit to grow and be sustained in our hearts. His face is our life source. We are the Father's plants within the earth. As we receive the light of Christ, we grow and produce the fruit of the Spirit. The marks of godliness appear. The production of fruit accelerates in our lives. Those fruits grow in the light that generously lends itself to us from His beautiful countenance.

But the fruit of the Spirit is love, joy, peace, longsuffering, gentleness, goodness, faith ...
—Galatians 5:22 (KJV)

The Scripture teaches that we are transformed as we simply behold Jesus. We don't have to strive and overextend ourselves. We don't have to toil in the spirit. We simply have to look to Jesus and receive.

But we all, with open face beholding as in a glass the glory of the Lord, are changed into the same image from glory to glory, even as by the Spirit of the Lord.
—2 Corinthians 3:18 (KJV)

As we behold His face, we are transformed into the beautiful image of Jesus. When we behold Him, we also behold His habits, His nature, and His countenance. We begin to familiarize ourselves with His peace, joy, patience, and overall goodness. And as we grow to emulate what we see in Him, we experience true maturity in spirit. Every moment we spend gazing at His beautiful face is a moment in which we are becoming more like the Master.

Our lives begin to reflect the brightness of His glory. Our behavior begins to model His example. Our beings become one with Him.

For God, who commanded the light to shine out of darkness, hath shined in our hearts, to give the light of the knowledge of the glory of God in the face of Jesus Christ.
—2 Corinthians 4:6 (KJV)

The countenance of Jesus's face brings illumination to your life. Look at His face and find your guiding light, and then allow that beautiful countenance to shine through you.

As children of the Lord, we are called to manifest His countenance through our entire beings—body, soul, and spirit. We are to be reflections of the marvelous light of His countenance. Beautiful Jesus shines like the sun, and He wants to shine through us in both word and deed.

We must reflect the Lord in both the natural and the spiritual.

In fact, I have encountered believers who were so close to Jesus that I could see a divine glow about their faces. I have been told on different occasions that my face was shining while I was preaching or coming out of private prayer time.

The glowing radiance of Jesus is within us, because Jesus is within us. But in order for the light in us to shine around us, we must remove the blockage. We must crucify the flesh and allow the brightness of Christ to radiate through us.

The countenance of Jesus, when it shines through, creates an atmosphere of God's glory all around us.

The more time we spend looking upon His face in worship, prayer, and study of the Word, the more we begin to glow.

Remember this spiritual rule: Every attribute about beautiful Jesus that we purposefully adore and purposefully praise will begin to manifest in us, body, soul, and spirit. So when you focus on His countenance, you begin to bear His image.

Everything around you becomes heavenly when you begin to bear the countenance of Christ. Angelic beings are drawn to His light, and demonic powers are dispelled by His light. His countenance brings peace and joy, deliverance and power, hope and assurance. You can be God's shining light in the earth, bringing the radiance of Christ everywhere you go.

PURPOSEFUL ADORATION:
HIS BEAUTIFUL COUNTENANCE

Jesus, I desire to look upon Your beautiful face. Your countenance, Your beaming and glorious light, has become my obsession. I want to see Your face. I want to know Your every feature. Jesus, Your face is beautiful. Let that same beauty and light shine forth from me. Instead of my face, Lord, I want others to see Yours.

CHAPTER 2

His Beautiful Head, Hair and Beard

His Beautiful Head

The beautiful head of Jesus reveals the story of the majestic Son of God who came from Heaven to earth to lavish His love upon us. The One Who made all things and held them together through the power of His mighty words had no place to lay His head.

Jesus said unto him, "The foxes have holes and the birds of the air have nests, but the Son of Man has nowhere to lay His head."
—Matthew 8:20 (NASB)

But at the cross, Jesus found a place to rest His divine head. When suffering upon that tree, He bowed His head, gave up His Spirit, and said "It is finished!" There in that moment, Jesus finally found rest for His beautiful head. He found rest for His head by loving us, dying for us, and purchasing our salvation.

So when Jesus had received the sour wine, He said, "It is finished!" And bowing His head, He gave up His spirit.
—John 19:30 (NKJV)

Jesus's head also speaks of His power over death, because usually, when people die, they give up their spirit and then rest their heads. But beautiful Jesus, doing it in reverse, first rested His head and then gave up His Spirit.

And today, the majestic and lovely head of Jesus reveals Him as the eternal King of Heaven Who is crowned with many crowns. The head that had nowhere to rest is now the head crowned with eternal glory.

His eyes were a flame of fire, and on His head were many crowns. He had a name written on Him that no one knew except Himself.
—Revelation 19:20 (NKJV)

The head of Jesus speaks of His unshakeable Kingdom and omnipotent authority. The crown of thorns was placed upon His head; the thorns found their way into His scalp. But where there was once a crown of thorns, there now rests an eternal crown of glory. He paid for our redemption and is now our eternal King. When you love the head of Jesus, you are telling the Lord Jesus His Kingdom endures forever and that nothing can ever dethrone Him.

Then I saw a white cloud, and seated on the cloud was someone like the Son of Man. He had a gold crown on his head and a sharp sickle in his hand.
—Revelation 14:14 (NLT)

His Beautiful Hair

The Bible declares that the head, hair, and clothes of Jesus are as white as snow.

His head and his hairs were white like wool, as white as snow; and his eyes were as a flame of fire ...
—Revelation 1:14 (KJV)

The whiteness speaks of His purity.

Her Nazarites were purer than snow, they were whiter than milk, they were more ruddy in body than rubies, their polishing was of sapphire ...
—Lamentations 4:7 (KJV)

The hair of Jesus reveals the purity of the spotless Lamb of God. He is purer than all who have come before Him and all who have and will come after Him. Everything about Him is pure: His life is pure, His mind is pure, His motives are pure, His words are pure. Everything about Jesus is pure, and He is the source of our purity.

The beautiful hair of Jesus being white like snow not only reveals His personal purity, but also His ability to purify any person who comes to Him for cleansing.

Come now, and let us reason together, saith the LORD: though your sins be as scarlet, they shall be as white as snow; though they be red like crimson, they shall be as wool.
—Isaiah 1:18 (KJV)

Cleanse me with hyssop, and I will be clean; wash me, and I will be whiter than snow.
—Psalm 51:7 (NIV)

Jesus is the sinless Savior Who washes us in His purifying blood. Jesus is our perfectly pure Lord Who washes our sins away. His hair being "white like snow" is also significant, because snow refers not only to purity, but also to the Word of God.

The rain and snow come down from the heavens
and stay on the ground to water the earth.
They cause the grain to grow,
producing seed for the farmer
and bread for the hungry.
It is the same with my word.
I send it out, and it always produces fruit.
It will accomplish all I want it to,
and it will prosper everywhere I send it.
—Isaiah 55:10-11 (NLT)

The Word of God refers to itself many times as "snow" and "water" which wash us clean. Snow comes down from above and melts to become the water we drink.

Just like snow, Jesus also came down from above to give us living water to drink. Jesus is the Word Who was made flesh. He came down from Heaven. He is the pure snow of God's Word and is now living water, given to us to drink. So the purity of His hair reveals His life-giving mission.

Jesus replied, "If you only knew the gift God has for you and who you are speaking to, you would ask me, and I would give you living water."
—John 4:10 (NLT)

And he said unto them, Ye are from beneath; I am from above: ye are of this world; I am not of this world.
—John 8:23 (KJV)

His beautiful hair is whiter than snow, in order to remind us that He is purity, God's Holy Word. And He is the One Who makes us clean. He doesn't just have impeccable purity; He is the source of it.

HIS BEAUTIFUL BEARD

The crown of Jesus's head and His hair present to us an image of how the power of God is distributed, from the top to the bottom. The hair on His head is the start of the flow of the anointing in our lives, because the oil is poured on top of the head. Jesus is our High Priest Who pours His Spirit upon our heads.

How wonderful and pleasant it is
*   when brothers live together in harmony!*
For harmony is as precious as the anointing oil
*   that was poured over Aaron's head,*
*   that ran down his beard*
*   and onto the border of his robe.*
—Psalm 133:1-2 (NLT)

The flow of the anointing oil begins at the top of the head. It flows from the hair down to the beard and then onto the robe. The anointing, the authority and power of God, begins with the Father and drips downward through Jesus to His servants.

So the hair of Jesus, the crown of His head, represents the giving of the Holy Spirit (symbolically, the pouring out of oil).

The Spirit was first poured upon Jesus during His baptism at the river Jordan, and a dove was seen over His head.

And Jesus, when he was baptized, went up straightway out of the water: and, lo, the heavens were opened unto him, and he saw the Spirit of God descending like a dove, and lighting upon him …
—Matthew 3:16 (KJV)

When the Holy Spirit first came upon the Church in the upper room (the baptism of fire), tongues of fire were seen upon the people's heads.

And there appeared unto them cloven tongues like as of fire, and it sat upon each of them.
—Acts 2:3 (KJV)

My point is this: The anointing and authority of God comes from above— from top to bottom. So before the anointing can touch the robe, it must cross over the bridge, which is the beard of Jesus.

The beard connects the flow of oil from the top of the head to the garment. The exact same fragrant oil poured upon Jesus by the Father is transferred to us by the conduit of His beard.

The general context of Psalm 133 is about the unity of the brethren. That unity is likened to Aaron the high priest and the application of the anointing oil which flows down his beard. But in that portion of scripture, God has placed a deeper truth about the beautiful beard of Jesus. That truth applies directly to the anointing flowing onto your life.

Aaron was the high priest to Israel, and Jesus is our heavenly High Priest. So Jesus stands before the Father to receive and impart the Holy Spirit on our behalf.

Seeing then that we have a great high priest, that is passed into the heavens, Jesus the Son of God, let us hold fast our profession.
—Hebrews 4:14 (KJV)

Now, the anointing oil which runs down Jesus's beard is called the "Precious Ointment." The ointment is "precious" because it symbolically represents the outpouring of the Holy Spirit—from the Father to Jesus and from Jesus to us.

Jesus prayed and asked the Father for the release of the Spirit.

And I will pray the Father, and he shall give you another Comforter, that he may abide with you for ever ...
—*John 14:16 (KJV)*

God has chosen to anoint His Son Jesus with the full measure of the Spirit. We receive that anointing through the bridge of His beard, as a result of His overflowing fullness. We know that only Jesus has the right to send the Holy Spirit to us and pour to His anointing upon our lives.

But when the Comforter is come, whom I will send unto you from the Father, even the Spirit of truth, which proceedeth from the Father, he shall testify of me.
—*John 15:26 (KJV)*

So the anointing oil "runs down" the beard of Jesus to His body—His Church. Jesus is our Head, and we are referred to as the Body of Christ (flesh of His flesh, bone of His bone). Jesus's beard transfers that precious oil to us.

The beard of Jesus is the bridge of the Holy Spirit by which the anointing oil rapidly and continuously flows from the Father, through the Son, to the Church. The power of the Spirit is exclusively, liberally, and intimately poured upon Jesus's head by God the Father without measure.

Picture the Father pouring the oil of the Spirit upon Jesus's head. That oil runs down His beard with haste and instantly touches your life when you surrender to Jesus by faith.

An Additional Benefit of the Beard

Yes, the beard of Jesus is the bridge of the anointing, but as powerful a truth as that is, the beard of Jesus comes with an additional benefit. Through His beautiful beard, the surrendered believer not only receives the anointing and the Holy Spirit, but also divine dignity and honor.

In Orthodox Jewish and Eastern cultures, the beard of a man represents honor. In the view of these ancient cultures, to pluck out someone's beard is the highest form of insult and disrespect. Many times throughout the Bible, we see the plucking out of the beard as a great sign of dishonor or even judgment that brings reproach.

He giveth his cheek to him that smiteth him: he is filled full with reproach.
—Lamentations 3:30 (KJV)

Looking now to the New Testament passion narrative, we see that Jesus becomes the willing recipient of this blatant and contemptuous disrespect. By letting His accusers pluck out His beard, Jesus took upon Himself His society's ultimate form of dishonor. His beard symbolizes His honor, which was maliciously stripped away.

His beard was violently plucked from His beautiful face so that we could live in His place of perfect honor before God. For us, Jesus willingly offered His beard to be torn from His face.

I offered my back to those who beat me
and my cheeks to those who pulled out my beard.
I did not hide my face
from mockery and spitting.
—Isaiah 50:6 (NLT)

In His deepest moments of suffering, Jesus followed the challenging demands of His own teaching to turn the other cheek, literally. He did not hide His face from the pain or disrespect. Driven by His unflinching love for you, He embraced the pain that came from the tearing of each hair that was uprooted from His cheeks. Having no hypocrisy, He did as He taught.

But I say unto you, That ye resist not evil: but whosoever shall smite thee
on thy right cheek, turn to him the other also.
—Matthew 5:39 (KJV)

Jesus gave His beard to be plucked by those who hated Him. In Eastern culture, to spit upon someone's face is also a sign of disrespect and dishonor. Jesus embraced this insult too.

The high priest and all of the chief priests, along with the elders and scribes, blindfolded Jesus and corporately covered His bleeding face with spittle.

And some began to spit on him, and to cover his face, and to buffet him,
and to say unto him, Prophesy: and the servants did strike him with the
palms of their hands.
—Mark 14:65 (KJV)

First they ripped out His majestic beard, stripping Him of His honor. Then they spit upon His face. Adding to their hateful actions, they proceeded to strike His bleeding, spittle-covered face with the palms of their hands. Jesus's holy face was completely covered in the spit of His creation. Afterward, six hundred Roman soldiers also spit upon Him and beat Him.

And they spit upon him, and took the reed, and smote him on the head.
—Matthew 27:30 (KJV)

Beautiful Jesus voluntarily gave His beard to be plucked and His face to be horrifically treated, in order to impart to us His own honor and glory. He took our shame, guilt, and dishonor to exchange them for His bright, shining face. He took the ugliness of our sin upon His face and gave us the glowing beauty and honor of it instead.

PURPOSEFUL ADORATION: HIS BEAUTIFUL HEAD, HAIR, AND BEARD

Beautiful Jesus, I love Your head, Your hair, and Your beard. Thank You
for wearing the crown of thorns upon Your lovely head so I can wear
a crown of glory in Heaven. Lord, I praise Your beautiful hair, which
reveals Your life-giving mission to bring salvation to my soul. Lord, I
pray the matchless honor and precious anointing that flows from Your
majestic beard would be imparted into my life as I adore You.

CHAPTER 3

HIS BEAUTIFUL EYES

When you want to connect with someone on a deeper level, you look into his or her eyes. Intimacy with Christ transpires when we look into His beautiful eyes. The Scripture tells us the Lord's eyes are like flames of fire.

His eyes were like flames of fire, and on his head were many crowns. A name was written on him that no one understood except himself.
—Revelation 19:12 (NLT)

Imagine His eyes.

They are like fire. They are burning, passionate, loving, piercing, beautiful eyes. When they look at you, they know you and love you. When Jesus fixes His gaze upon you, the attention of the great divine Mind is yours.

Through His sight, Jesus was overcome with compassion for the lost and the broken.

When he saw the crowds, he had compassion on them because they were confused and helpless, like sheep without a shepherd.
—Matthew 9:36 (NLT)

"When He saw the crowds." Think about that phrase!

His eyes are filled with compassion, because they see every need, they know every broken part of the human condition. With His eyes, He sees the needs of humanity, and compassion fills Him. With His eyes, He can see sickness, hunger, demonic oppression, and sin. Because of what He saw, Jesus healed the sick, drove out demons, miraculously fed the multitudes, and selflessly laid down His own life.

Jesus looked at the lepers. Jesus looked at Jairus. Jesus looked at the blind beggar. Jesus looked at people through His beautiful eyes. In one instance the Scripture records, Jesus looked upon a rich young ruler.

Looking at him, Jesus felt a love for him and said to him, "One thing you lack: go and sell all you possess and give to the poor, and you will have treasure in heaven; and come, follow Me."
—Matthew 10:21 (NASB)

Jesus looked at him and loved him. Jesus would be denied by the same man who chose his earthly riches over Jesus. But Jesus still looked at Him with love. He gave that same tender look to everyone who came to Him. Whether they would later accept or reject Him was no matter, for He looked at them with love.

He has not changed. Today, He still sees through the same loving eyes. He looks at you with eyes of mercy, compassion, tenderness, and love. He looks about the earth with a fervent, unquenchable love. He searches for anyone who, with faith and not doubting, will call upon Him. He searches to see to whom He can reveal Himself.

With those same loving, compassionate eyes, Jesus also purifies by means of examination. The same eyes which recognize our needs and weaknesses also perceive our thoughts and witness our every action and motive.

But when Jesus perceived their thoughts, he answering said unto them, "What reason ye in your hearts?"
—Luke 5:22 (KJV)

The eyes of Jesus have a purifying effect in that they pierce to the very core of our beings. Jesus perceives every thought and clearly sees all the nuances—good and evil—that make up your person. Only the eyes of Jesus can see every thought, motive, and action. Therefore, Jesus is the only One Who can rightfully judge the earth.

Now if any man build upon this foundation gold, silver, precious stones, wood, hay, stubble; Every man's work shall be made manifest: for the day shall declare it, because it shall be revealed by fire; and the fire shall try every man's work of what sort it is. If any man's work abide which he hath built thereupon, he shall receive a reward.
—1 Corinthians 3:12-14 (KJV)

At the end of all things, the Lord Himself will judge the works of every man and every woman. Depending upon the foundation of those works and the motives behind them, the works will either remain or dissolve in judgment.

"… it shall be revealed by fire …"

What is that fire which separates the corruptible from the incorruptible? What is this blaze that burns away all false works and motives? What purifying heat will reveal the precious things that remain eternally? That fire is the sight of the Lord. His eyes of fire are the flames that shall test every work. Everything shall be revealed by the fire of His eyes.

The LORD is in His holy temple,
The LORD's throne is in heaven;
His eyes behold,
His eyelids test the sons of men.
—Psalm 11:4 (KJV)

Only the eyes of Jesus can see the true intentions veiled behind man's every action. He sees the motive behind every word and deed.

For the ways of man are before the eyes of the Lord, and he pondereth all his goings.
—Proverbs 5:21 (KJV)

The eyes of the Lord are in every place, beholding the evil and the good.
—Proverbs 15:3 (KJV)

When the Lord looked down upon the wickedness of men, He beheld that which grieved Him. The world was weighed under His righteous judgment, and God decided to flood the whole earth.

However, Noah found grace in the eyes of the Lord.

But Noah found grace in the eyes of the LORD.
—*Genesis 6:8 (KJV)*

We too have found grace in the eyes of Lord through the shed blood of Jesus. We have His protection from wrath and destruction. We have found grace in the eyes of our loving Savior.

The eyes of the Lord are upon the righteous, and his ears are open unto their cry.
—*Psalm 34:15 (KJV)*

His beautiful eyes are forever fixed upon His people. The Lord looks upon us with the intention to care for us and bless us. He lovingly watches over you, joyfully planning His every good gift toward you and vigilantly protecting you from harm. He watches for the enemy, and He prevents destruction. He watches for opportunities to grace you, and He guides you into blessings. His attention is fixed on you.

For thus saith the LORD of hosts; After the glory hath he sent me unto the nations which spoiled you: for he that toucheth you toucheth the apple of his eye.
—*Zechariah 2:8 (KJV)*

Jesus can't get enough of you, because He loves you. He observes and appreciates every detail about your life. His eyes are all-powerful, all-knowing eyes that are looking out for your best interests.

With our limited perception, we are only able to make judgments based upon actions and words. However, by worshipping the image of Jesus, by adoring His beautiful eyes, we activate His insightful and knowing discernment. We gain supernatural perception through the worship of Jesus.

When we see through the beautiful eyes of Jesus, we begin to recognize and avoid pitfalls and traps laid for us by our adversary. We can even avoid the snares of men. When we look with His perception, we see beyond the natural and gain insight we otherwise would have missed.

PURPOSEFUL ADORATION:
HIS BEAUTIFUL EYES

Jesus, look at me with Your beautiful eyes. See me, search me, and know me. Captivate me, weigh me, and purify me. I long to be locked into Your inescapable gaze. When I look into Your eyes, I can see Who You are. I can see Your love, mercy, compassion, and righteousness. Lord, I can sense it all so intensely when I look into Your beautiful eyes.

CHAPTER 4

His Beautiful Ears

It was a rainy Sunday night. After attending a powerful service at church, I was driving on Highway 73 to my home in Southern California. My car was brand new and should have had no issues. Yet, out of nowhere, my car began to overheat. It went haywire! The system's alerts began to sound chaotically. The car began to lose its forward momentum. I pressed the gas harder to make up for the fading momentum, but there was no power. The engine was revving, but I just was not moving forward like normal. My car slowly stalled, so I had to pull over. And there I was, in the middle of the freeway, on a rainy night. I didn't know what to do.

I wish I could tell you my soul was still. However, my first reaction was one of frustration. I just began to say out loud, "Why? Why? Why? Why is this happening?!" Cutting through my frustration, the still, small voice of the Lord calmed me and said, "Don't worry. I'm in this." That little nudge from the Lord brought stillness to me. His voice has a calming effect, you know? After all, He was the one who spoke to the storm and calmed it.

So I got out of my car to survey the scene. It was actually quite nice being stuck on the hills of the 73 in the rain. I know that doesn't sound nice, but it was, in a strange way.

I called a tow truck, and my car was taken to the dealership to get repaired.

Fast forward roughly two weeks. I went to the dealership to pick up my car. I was still curious what exactly had gone wrong with my vehicle. I was wandering around the dealership thinking, "Why am I even here? What happened with this car? This is odd." Still, I was walking in that peace-filled assurance from the Lord I received when He told me, "Don't worry. I'm in this."

I went to one of the desks to pick up my paperwork. I was told to go outside and that my car would be pulled around the corner to my right. I was familiar with that dealership, because I had been there before. I knew where to go.

However, as I began to walk to where my car was to meet me, I began to feel a sensation of heat rest upon my ears. I knew in my spirit that the ears of the Lord were being activated. He could hear something, and He was allowing me to listen.

The Lord instructed me, "Turn left; don't turn right."

I don't know how else to word this, but I am telling you: His ears were guiding me.

So I turned left and found myself in an empty room. I looked around the room and saw no one. The Lord said, "Look." I said to the Lord, "There's nobody here." The Lord simply said it again. "Look".

My attention was drawn to the corner of the room. There I saw a hidden crevice between a large storage unit and the wall.

And in that crevice, a man was sitting in a chair—dying in his sleep, choking on his vomit.

I looked more intently to make sure I was actually seeing what I was seeing. It was, indeed, a man sitting on a chair. His head was tilted back. He was completely asleep. And he was choking on his own vomit with nobody else in sight.

I tapped his shoulder to try to wake him, but he did not respond. In the spirit, I could see his soul about to slip into Hell. So I grabbed the man and shook him. I almost tossed him against the wall. He fell down on his face. And when he fell down on his face, his throat was cleared of his vomit. He remained on the floor, as I ran out of the room and yelled for someone to call an ambulance.

I ran back to the man and pulled him up by his shirt. I rested him against the wall and asked him, "What's wrong? What's going on?" I could smell alcohol on him. His breath reeked of hard liquor. It was the middle of the day, and that man was as drunk as could be while he was at work!

In a drunken stupor, he had fallen asleep on a chair with his head tilted back and had choked on his own vomit. He would have died if not for the ears of the Lord hearing His struggling. I told the man, "Jesus saved you! Jesus saved you! You can turn to Him. You need to turn to Him."

He began to plead with me to not tell anyone there, because he didn't want to lose his job. I shared the Gospel with him, and we parted ways.

Finally, I got into my car. The instant I started to drive away, I remembered the words of the Lord: "Don't worry. I'm in this."

The Lord had allowed my car to break down two weeks earlier so He could save that man from dying.

It was the ears of the Lord that had worked through me, allowing me to hear the voice of the Father. Jesus hears the Father, and when we submit ourselves to the Lord, we can hear the Father through the ears of Jesus.

Not only do the ears of Beautiful Jesus hear the Father, but His ears are also attentive to us.

What a wonderful truth, that we can have the attention of the Lord. The Scripture asks us a rhetorical question concerning God's ability to hear us.

Is he deaf—the one who made your ears? Is he blind—the one who formed your eyes?
—Psalm 94:9 (NLT)

The Son of God is able to hear you. Seated at the right hand of the Father, Jesus is capable of hearing and answering your prayers. He is the Mediator between you and the Father, so He must possess the divine ability to hear all who come before Him asking in worship.

For there is only one God and one Mediator who can reconcile God and humanity—the man Christ Jesus.
—1 Timothy 2:5 (NLT)

Think about how truly amazing this is: That Jesus can, all at once, hear your prayers and the prayers of all who call upon His name. Millions of voices are raised toward Heaven producing hundreds of millions of prayers, perhaps billions. Yet Beautiful Jesus is able to hear every single one of those requests.

Ask, and it shall be given you; seek, and ye shall find; knock, and it shall be opened unto you.
—Matthew 7:7 (KJV)

I tell you, you can pray for anything, and if you believe that you've received it, it will be yours.
—Mark 11:24 (NLT)

His beautiful ears can hear you. All you have to do is approach Him by faith or in faith. Jesus often told people their healings, their miracles, and the answers to their prayers were results of their faith in Him. Answered prayer, according to the Lord, is a result of faith. That faith is only produced by looking at the Son of God.

When healing the blind, He spoke this truth.

Then he touched their eyes and said, "Because of your faith, it will happen."
—Matthew 9:29 (NLT)

When healing the centurion's servant, He taught the same.

And Jesus said unto the centurion, "Go thy way; and as thou hast believed, so be it done unto thee." And his servant was healed in the selfsame hour.
—Matthew 8:13 (KJV)

Time and time again, Jesus reiterated this principle of receiving according to faith in His ability to perform.

"You don't have enough faith," Jesus told them. "I tell you the truth, if you had faith even as small as a mustard seed, you could say to this mountain, 'Move from here to there,' and it would move. Nothing would be impossible."
—Matthew 17:20 (NLT)

Then Jesus said to the disciples, "Have faith in God. I tell you the truth, you can say to this mountain, 'May you be lifted up and thrown into the sea,' and it will happen. But you must really believe it will happen and have no doubt in your heart. I tell you, you can pray for anything, and if you believe that you've received it, it will be yours."
—Mark 11:22-24 (NLT)

The Lord answered, "If you had faith even as small as a mustard seed, you could say to this mulberry tree, 'May you be uprooted and thrown into the sea,' and it would obey you!"
—Luke 17:6 (NLT)

Jesus heard, and then acted according to the faith of the people who approached Him. I think of the blind beggar who caught the attention of Jesus through the sound of desperate pleadings! He desperately called out to the One Who could make him whole by yelling his plea!

So he began shouting, "Jesus, Son of David, have mercy on me!"
—Luke 18:38 (NLT)

Jesus heard the desperate cries of faith from a broken man through His beautiful ears. Whenever people approached Jesus, they presented to Him their cases. They would tell of their suffering, their sickness, and their struggles. And Jesus, attentive and kind, would hear them out. They would involve Him in their situation by telling Him what they desired more than anything else. They spoke their needy prayers into His loving ears, and He moved according to their faith.

And the Lord will do the same for you. He wants you to approach Him. He wants you to tell Him about all you need. Otherwise, why would the Scriptures encourage us to ask?

Don't worry about anything; instead, pray about everything. Tell God
what you need, and thank him for all he has done.
—Philippians 4:6 (NLT)

He wants to turn His ears to you, because He loves to hear the voice of His beloved people praising and adoring His name. Worship King Jesus, and His pleasure will cause Him to give you His attention as you present your request before Him.

The secret is to "ask in faith" after a significant time of worship and love. Pour out the sacrifice of praise. Let the sound of your adoration fill His ears. Delight in Him through praise, and let Him delight in you through hearing and fulfilling your requests.

To some degree, we could say Jesus has selective hearing.

Soon a violent windstorm came up, and the waves were breaking over the boat, so that it was being swamped. But Jesus was in the stern, sleeping on the cushion. So they woke Him and said, "Teacher, don't You care that we are perishing?" Then Jesus got up and rebuked the wind and the sea. "Silence!" He commanded. "Be still!" And the wind died down, and it was perfectly calm.
—*Mark 4:37-39 (BSB)*

Jesus chose not to hear all the noise of the storm. He slept through a violent windstorm. He slept through the tumultuous waves pounding over what seemed to the disciples a sinking boat. The disciples thought they were dying and cried out in fear. Jesus immediately arose to address their cries. Jesus is always attentive to the voice of His beloved people. They approached Jesus in hopes that He could do something. And Jesus responded by calming the storm.

Be confident that Jesus hears and answers your prayers. His ears are eternally attentive to your cries and supplications. He loves answering when you call, but even more, He longs to hear your cries of adoration toward His ears.

During difficult or impossible times, turn your focus away from the storm and upon the tender and attentive ears of Jesus. Let your words be full of adoration. Know that He is ready to hear and answer the prayers that fall upon His beautiful ears.

He is not deaf. He is not disconnected. He hears you. He loves you, and He is attentive to your faith-filled voice.

PURPOSEFUL ADORATION: HIS BEAUTIFUL EARS

Beautiful Jesus, I thank You for Your attentive ears. I thank You that they receive my prayers and my praise. I love Your beautiful ears which gracefully receive my desperate and pressing prayers. Thank You that as I purposefully adore Your beautiful ears, I receive Your attention. Thank You, Jesus, for Your beautiful ears.

CHAPTER 5

HIS BEAUTIFUL NOSE

Have you ever come across a random scent that reminded you of your childhood, a trip to some foreign part of the world, or a loved one? The sense of smell is linked with memory. Scent has the power to bring about a memory long forgotten and take you to places from your past. Whether a scent triggers a pleasant or painful memory, it has the power to place you in moments from your former days. Scent, therefore, has the ability to invoke, along with memories, strong emotions—good and bad.

Knowing the powerful connection between scent and memory, pay close attention to this verse:

And when he took the scroll, the four living beings and the twenty-four elders fell down before the Lamb. Each one had a harp, and they held gold bowls filled with incense, which are the prayers of God's people.
—Revelation 5:8 (NLT)

Obviously, the Lord does not rely upon physical scent to access His memories. He is constantly aware of all things—past, present, and future. But there is something to be said about the Bible's correlation between prayer and incense. I take it to mean the Lord is mindful of the requests you present to Him. Not a single one of your prayers, which arises before the beautiful nose of Jesus, is forgotten.

Let my prayer be set forth, before thee as incense, and lifting up of my hands as the evening sacrifice.
—*Psalm 141:2 (KJV)*

Our prayers are as incense in the nostrils of our Lord Jesus. He breathes in your prayer requests, your worship, and your praise as incense. Your prayers are the incense offered by the elders who are mentioned in the Book of Revelation. Playing their harps, the elders offer your prayers as incense to Jesus. They present your needs before the Lord when they fall down before Him and give purposeful adoration to the Lamb.

Often I pray things like, "Beautiful Jesus, breathe in my purposeful adoration of You. It is the sweet aroma of incense in the golden censers of the elders which brings the greatest pleasure to Your soul."

When Jesus inhales your prayers, He can discern every word. He can even sense all the sorrow found within your every tear. Yes, every tear you've shed for that lost loved one, every need, every desire—He sees it, He inhales it, He senses it. He can identify with the pain you are facing when you pray. And Jesus has promised to answer the faith-filled prayers of His saints.

When Jesus breathes in the incense of our prayers through His nose, our requests—our deepest desires and adoration—go directly into His divine mind, where He begins to process and formulate His good plans of peace toward our requests. He then breathes out the Word of the Lord, and the angels dispatch blessings on our behalf to fulfill His decree.

Every type of incense has a distinct aroma that rises before the throne of Jesus. Each prayer is unique. Every expression of praise and adoration is unique.

The Lord breathes in and smells our prayers as incense. His all-knowing mind sees our situation, and His memory bank activates on our behalf. In His eternal memory is forever stored His victorious triumph over sin and death. He vividly remembers being tempted in all points and overcoming for us.

For we have not a High Priest which cannot sympathize with the feeling of our infirmities; but was in all points tempted as we are, yet without sin. Let us therefore come boldly unto the throne of grace, that we may obtain mercy.
—Hebrews 4:15-16 (KJV)

He remembers being the mighty Warrior Who defeated Satan at the cross. Being aware of His own power, remembering His victories, He moves to become victorious in your circumstance. Now He has become our Power, so He activates His might on our behalf to save us.

But everything starts with the aroma of incense that rises before Him and enters into His holy nostrils.

He sympathizes, and He alone can save us. Beautiful Jesus hears our prayers with His ears, but He inhales our prayers as incense through His nose—and He always answers us through His various features.

Our prayers and purposeful adoration are incense offered before Him. Jesus breathes in the cry of your heart, and He can identify with your struggle. He remembers the feeling of being tempted in all points and remaining victorious and perfect through every trial. He was found "without sin" and blameless. That is why He sympathizes with us, and He has promised to answer your prayers and whatsoever you ask in His name.

Realize your access into Jesus and present your requests with confidence. We can offer many forms of incense before the Lord that is received by His beautiful nose. He breathes in what you offer to Him, and He breathes out your answer.

Then the LORD said to Moses, "Gather fragrant spices—resin droplets, mollusk shell, and galbanum—and mix these fragrant spices with pure frankincense, weighed out in equal amounts. Using the usual techniques of the incense maker, blend the spices together and sprinkle them with salt to produce a pure and holy incense. Grind some of the mixture into a very fine powder and put it in front of the Ark of the Covenant, where I will meet with you in the Tabernacle. You must treat this incense as most holy. Never use this formula to make this incense for yourselves. It is reserved for the LORD, and you must treat it as holy."
—*Exodus 30:34-37 (NLT)*

In this chapter, it is not my goal to break down the symbolic meaning of each ingredient mentioned in the above portion of scripture. I simply want to point out the fact that the Lord was very specific in how He instructed Moses and the priests to create the incense to be offered in worship. What God showed Moses and the Levites reflects the specificity He requires in our worship. God does not receive just anything that comes before Him. What He requires is specific. You could say the Lord has very particular tastes.

While I don't want to focus on the different ingredients used in the Tabernacle incense, I do want to focus on the different "ingredients" offered in our own spiritual blend of heavenly incense—what we offer daily to the Lamb of God.

Every communication we offer to the Lord is incense that rises up into His nostrils. Just as every kind of incense (and ingredient) has its own unique scent, so our prayers, in every form and kind, have varying scents. Yes, every kind of spiritual incense has a distinct aroma that rises before the throne of the Lord. He breathes in your prayer requests and your worship as incense.

So what are you offering to the Lord? What are the ingredients of your worship?

BREATH

God gave you the breath of life. He wants you to use it to praise His holy name.

Let everything that has breath praise the Lord.
—Psalm 150:6 (NIV)

Furthermore, when you were born again, you received another breath—the breath of the Spirit. This is the very same which proceeded out of the lungs of Jesus.

And when he had said this, he breathed on them, and saith unto them, "Receive ye the Holy Ghost."
—John 20:22 (KJV)

Only through the breath of the Spirit can we can correctly offer worship to Jesus. We practice purposeful adoration through the Spirit and by the Spirit.

Your breath is your life and your offering unto the Lord. When you offer your breath to the Lord, you are, by the Spirit, using what God put into you to give adoration back to Him. When you put your breath into your adoration, you are offering yourself as a worship offering to the Lord. Breath is an ingredient of your spiritual incense of worship.

FAITH

Without faith, we cannot approach God, know God, or please God in any way.

But without faith it is impossible to please him: for he that cometh to God must believe that he is, and that he is a rewarder of them that diligently seek him.
—Hebrews 11:6 (KJV)

Think then about just how important faith is. Faith is a key ingredient to creating the sweet-smelling aroma of purposeful adoration. Worship and faith go hand in hand, for you must believe in God the Father before you can sincerely offer worship to Him. It was by faith that Jacob was able to offer unto the Lord the worship He was due.

It was by faith that Jacob, when he was old and dying, blessed each of Joseph's sons and bowed in worship as he leaned on his staff.
—Hebrews 11:21 (NLT)

Faith is a crucial ingredient of your spiritual incense of worship.

LOVE

The Holy Spirit pours His love into our hearts so we can worship and love Jesus. The Father and the Holy Spirit love Jesus immeasurably, and only through God's love can we truly love Jesus correctly.

And this hope will not lead to disappointment. For we know how dearly God loves us, because he has given us the Holy Spirit to fill our hearts with his love.
—Romans 5:5 (NLT)

When we allow love to flow through our hearts, by the Holy Spirit, we are fulfilling God's greatest commandment:

Jesus said to him, "You shall love the LORD your God with all your heart, with all your soul, and with all your mind."
—Mathew 22:37 (KJV)

Love is an ingredient of your spiritual incense of worship.

PRAISE

Praise is the verbal expression of adoration for God, His nature, and His powerful actions. Offering praise to Jesus glorifies Him, and that is the key that unlocks the door to the throne room. Praise brings about revelation.

Whoso offereth praise glorifieth me: and to him that ordereth his conversation aright will I shew the salvation of God.
—*Psalm 50:23 (KJV)*

Praise is an ingredient of your spiritual incense of worship.

WORSHIP

Our breath, faith, love, and praise are all gathered together and received by the Lord as a fragrant aroma of worship. Of course, there are many "ingredients" to worship that I did not cover in this section, but I want you to know this truth: The beautiful nose of Jesus breathes in and smells the aroma of what you offer in worship.

Worship is the intoxicating incense that draws Christ unto us. The more spice of worship we add to our prayers, the greater the pull the aroma will have on His beautiful nose.

But the hour cometh, and now is, when the true worshippers shall worship the Father in spirit and in truth: for the Father seeketh such to worship him.
—*John 4:23 (KJV)*

We must worship in the Spirit, not in the flesh.

What Do You Offer Him?

We can add various different amounts of different ingredients to the incense we offer to the Lord. In doing so, we create for Him our own unique offering. And the aroma of what we create can vary; it can even be unpleasant. Imagine if your mixture of prayer contained only needs, requests, and desires mixed with faith. We need to mix in the ingredients of worship, so that our incense will not become bitter in the beautiful nose of Jesus. Different amounts of different ingredients create different aromas.

As it goes with your prayer life, there are different kinds of incense you can offer to the Lord.

1. Sweet
2. Mid-level
3. Low-Level
4. Strange

Sweet

Do you offer Him the sweet-smelling incense? This is the pure aroma of purposeful adoration. The Bible speaks of the sweet incense (which the Lord loves).

And he made the holy anointing oil, and the pure incense of sweet spices, according to the work of the apothecary.
—Exodus 37:29 (KJV)

We should often offer to Him the pure act of purposeful adoration with the ingredients of worship, without "self," needs, or wants added.

MID-LEVEL

Do you offer Him mid-level incense? This is incense mixed with some of God and some of self. This is the incense of the prayer request. We tend to focus on Jesus, then turn our focus, prayers, and motives back to self. This is not evil. In fact, the prayer request is helpful. But this is not the best we can offer Him.

Of course, there is nothing wrong with offering prayer requests. However, we must primarily offer Him the sweet-smelling incense.

LOW-LEVEL

Do you offer Him low-level incense? When our worship and prayer is completely revolving around self, we offer the Lord the lowest kind of incense. In His mercy, He does not turn His face from us. Instead, He endures the unpleasant scents of self. This is when we pray with fear, doubt, pride, and anxiety. We must learn to not offer this kind of incense.

STRANGE

Do you offer to Him strange incense? This type of incense actually gets the attention of the demonic realm, because it is sensual and it used by the occult.

Beware of incantation offered out of a manipulative heart—the kind of incantation that disguises itself as prayer. This sort we should never, ever attempt to offer to the Lord.

And Nadab and Abihu, the sons of Aaron, took either of them his censer, and put fire therein, and put incense thereon, and offered strange fire before the LORD, which he commanded them not.
—Leviticus 10:1 (KJV)

CONCLUSION

You can give strange, low-level, mid-level or sweet-smelling incense to the Lord. The choice is yours.

The purest form of incense is free of from selfish ambition. Again, I emphasize that prayer requests are not evil, but they must not make up the entirety of your prayer life. In fact, Jesus has promised to answer the faith-filled prayers of His saints. When Jesus breathes in the incense of your prayers through His beautiful nose, your requests and deepest desires go directly into His divine mind, where He begins to process and formulate His good plans of peace toward your requests. He then breathes out the Word of the Lord, and the angels dispatch on your behalf to fulfill the Lord's decree. So, yes, offer Him the incense of request (mid-level). But also remember this: We should desire to go deeper by pleasing Him through our worship.

It is best to most often offer to the Lord the sweetest of incense. The ingredients of our incense mix together into different types of combinations of incense that we offer to Jesus. Purposeful adoration, that intentional worshipping of His Person that I have described throughout this book, is the greatest incense we can offer. It is incense crafted only from our love for Him—the ingredients gathered from what we see and adore in Him.

When Jesus inhales your prayers, He can discern every word. He can smell every need, every desire. And He can identify with the pain you are facing when you pray.

Jesus's presence is drawn to us when we offer prayers of purposeful adoration because our lives become the most pleasing aroma of love to Him. The highest level of incense, the sweetest smelling aroma to our High Priest, Jesus, is purposeful adoration. Purposeful adoration is the sweetest savor of incense to Jesus. The greatest prayer we can pray is purposeful adoration.

Remember that smell is associated with emotions and memories. When you practice purposeful adoration, Jesus associates your face with the highest levels of His pleasure. So every time He thinks about your face, He remembers you are someone who brings the greatest pleasure to His heart. Of course, He loves all His children, but He does not have memories of all His children practicing purposeful adoration.

THE ALTAR OF PURPOSEFUL ADORATION

Our life is an altar on which we offer up the incense of purposeful adoration toward Jesus. The aroma will rise upward from your body and into the nostrils of Jesus, attracting the presence of His Holy Spirit to you. God dwells and lingers in the praises of His people. When we perform purposeful adoration, the aroma of our worship arises and the presence of the Lord descends upon our altar of adoration.

Jesus is attracted to the scent of your purposeful adoration, because it brings Him the ultimate pleasure: Jesus discerns purposeful adoration in the incense and descends upon your life with glory and power.

When Beautiful Jesus smells a life of purposeful adoration emanating from you, He becomes attracted to your presence. He loves to be near those who practice purposeful adoration often, because the aroma of sweet incense has the most pleasing scent to His beautiful nose.

He loves inhaling the incense of purposeful adoration emanating from His saints. When you continually offer this incense for Jesus to breathe in, the manifest presence of Holy Spirit will be very near to you. Angels will be dwelling around you constantly. His manifest presence will be very near to you at all times. Jesus will be intimately drawn to you, and He will become eternally invested into everything you are and everything you do in life.

The saints who practice purposeful adoration remind Jesus of His greatest pleasure and joy. Think about this: Your purposeful adoration was a part of the "joy that was set before Him" when He endured the cross, despising the shame.

Looking unto Jesus the author and finisher of our faith; who for the joy that was set before him endured the cross, despising the shame, and is set down at the right hand of the throne of God.
—Hebrews 12:2 (KJV)

PURPOSEFUL ADORATION: HIS BEAUTIFUL NOSE

Beautiful Jesus, I thank You for Your beautiful nose, which receives the incense of my purposeful adoration, my worship. Help me to master the art of offering sweet incense to You. Let my prayers and worship be made of faith, love, praise, and breath. I want the sweet aroma of the highest worship to fill Your throne room and intoxicate You with my love. Let my life be the altar from which the finest incense of worship is continually offered.

CHAPTER 6

HIS BEAUTIFUL MOUTH

Time and again, the Scripture tells us when Jesus sat down to teach, He would open His beautiful mouth.

And he opened his mouth, and taught them, saying …
—*Matthew 5:2 (KJV)*

From the mouth of the Lord come truth, wisdom, and revelation. Jesus, full of the wisdom of Heaven, would teach spiritual truths. Many times, the meanings of those truths were hidden from his listeners' understanding. There was, indeed, great depth to the words of Jesus. And that depth often could often only be forded successfully with divine aid. Sometimes, the meaning of His words had to be revealed by the Holy Spirit. However, there was also a unique simplicity to the way He spoke. With parables, Jesus masterfully communicated the mysteries of Heaven in earthly terms. In His simple yet in-depth teachings, Jesus was able to speak to everyone, no matter where they were on their journey toward God.

His words are so simple and, at the same time, so deep, that they can be understood for their immediate meaning and explored further for their hidden treasures. But it wasn't just revelation that flowed from the beautiful mouth of Jesus.

The mouth of Jesus was also the same that spit upon dirt to heal a blind man.

Then he spit on the ground, made mud with the saliva, and spread the mud over the blind man's eyes. He told him, "Go wash yourself in the pool of Siloam." (Siloam means "sent.") So the man went and washed and came back seeing!
—John 9:6-7 (NLT)

Out of the mouth of Jesus also came His beautiful voice, which is described as being like "many waters."

And I heard a voice from heaven, as the voice of many waters, and as the voice of a great thunder: and I heard the voice of harpers harping with their harps ...
—Revelation 14:2 (KJV)

His mouth carries the voice that is like many waters—the waters of love, peace, and blessings. This rushing water is flowing toward you, bringing with it refreshing and life. Waves of glory and love will wash over you when the Lord projects His vibrant voice in your direction. This water will wash away all doubt and worry.

The beautiful mouth of Jesus also released the breath of the Lord.

And when he had said this, he breathed on them, and saith unto them, "Receive ye the Holy Ghost ..."
—John 20:22 (KJV)

Jesus breathes the breath of life, the essence of the Spirit, out of His beautiful mouth. If ever you need strength, if ever you need to be uplifted, just begin to worship and adore the beautiful mouth of Jesus.

Allow the Lord to breathe upon you and speak over you. Then, with the faith of a child, breathe deeply and be filled with all that comes from His divine breath. His lips are truly the gates out of which the Spirit comes rushing. His breath is the vehicle that carries the Spirit. This fulfills the Word that was decreed from His own lips:

"He shall glorify me: for he shall receive of mine, and shall shew it unto you."
—John 16:14 (KJV)

When Jesus speaks, the Spirit moves.

With His voice, He also makes declarations that carry the weight of divine authority. His voice is a powerful force, unstoppable and impossible to resist. Paul the Apostle, in his final days of being Saul the persecutor, was knocked off his horse when Jesus spoke.

As he was approaching Damascus on this mission, a light from heaven suddenly shone down around him. He fell to the ground and heard a voice saying to him, "Saul! Saul! Why are you persecuting me?" "Who are you, lord?" Saul asked. And the voice replied, "I am Jesus, the one you are persecuting! Now get up and go into the city, and you will be told what you must do."
—Acts 9:3-6 (NLT)

I do not believe Jesus was speaking out of anger in Acts 9. He was speaking out of His love for the Church. When He confronted Saul, Jesus spoke from grace. His voice is a wave of divine love.

The Master's voice sent out vibrations of love and mercy. These vibrations were so profoundly powerful that Saul immediately submitted to the Lord's commands when He said, "Now get up and go ..."

And that wasn't the only instance when those who opposed the Lord were subjected to the power of His voice. In the garden of Gethsemane, while Jesus was being arrested, the five hundred soldiers fell backward to the ground at the utterance of His simple words.

As soon then as he had said unto them, "I am he," they went backward, and fell to the ground.
—John 18:6 (KJV)

Why hadn't people fallen under the weight of the glory of His words before then? It's because He can willingly direct the force of His voice through His words.

The power of His voice goes beyond influence over men. He even commands the material world—all of nature. His voice stopped a storm in the middle of its rage.

When Jesus woke up, he rebuked the wind and said to the waves, "Silence! Be still!" Suddenly the wind stopped, and there was a great calm. Then he asked them, "Why are you afraid? Do you still have no faith?" The disciples were absolutely terrified. "Who is this man?" they asked each other. "Even the wind and waves obey him!"
—Mark 4:39-41 (NLT)

His voice calmed the storms then, and His voice can calm the storms in your life today.

His voice also carries divine healing. Yes, divine healing also comes through His touch. But His voice is just as divine as His hands. By His voice alone, He commanded the healing of the centurion's servant.

"I am not even worthy to come and meet you. Just say the word from where you are, and my servant will be healed. I know this because I am under the authority of my superior officers, and I have authority over my soldiers. I only need to say, 'Go,' and they go, or 'Come,' and they come. And if I say to my slaves, 'Do this,' they do it." When Jesus heard this, he was amazed. Turning to the crowd that was following him, he said, "I tell you, I haven't seen faith like this in all Israel!" And when the officer's friends returned to his house, they found the slave completely healed.
—Luke 7:7-10 (NLT)

The voice of Jesus carries the power for the miraculous. Waves of power would leave His beautiful mouth to make people whole! The mouth of Jesus spoke with the same divine and creative authority that backed the words of the Father when He spoke the world into existence. Everything that now exists is held together based upon what He has spoken.

The Son radiates God's own glory and expresses the very character of God, and he sustains everything by the mighty power of his command.

*When he had cleansed us from our sins, he sat down in the place of honor
at the right hand of the majestic God in heaven.*
—*Hebrews 1:3 (NLT)*

That's true authority. That's true power. All the universe is held together
by the command of Christ, the very Word of God.

This reminds me of a cosmological theory. "String theory" suggests that
every object in existence is held together by tiny, vibrating strings. This
"vibration" is what holds all reality in place.

I think it could very well be that these vibrations are the eternal effects
of God's command that brought everything into being. In other words,
the voice of Jesus is what holds all things in place—just as the book of
Hebrews tells us!

... he sustains everything by the mighty power of his command ...
—*Hebrews 1:3 (NLT)*

This sort of thinking opens our minds to properly consider the largeness
of Christ's voice, its actual abilities. His voice, which is released by His
mouth, has much more to it than we could ever possibly imagine.

Consider this popular Bible verse:

*A good man out of the good treasure of his heart bringeth forth that which
is good; and an evil man out of the evil treasure of his heart bringeth forth
that which is evil: for of the abundance of the heart his mouth speaketh.*
—*Luke 6:45 (KJV)*

The Bible teaches that one speaks from what abounds in the heart. It isn't a mystery, then, why Jesus spoke with such effectiveness and such authority. What vastness is in His heart? It is the same that is expressed in the authority of His voice, moved through His beautiful mouth. His mouth expresses His heart. Out of His mouth flow love, power, wisdom, mystery, and so much more.

And with that same mouth, the Lord also gives to us the ultimate reward for all we do in His name: His beautiful smile. Knowing that one has pleased the Lord is true spiritual satisfaction.

May the Lord smile on you
  and be gracious to you.
—Numbers 6:25 (NLT)

Jesus warns us that those who are apathetic about the matters of the spirit will be spewed from His mouth—away from oneness with Him. This means, conversely, that those who are passionate about Him will remain in Him and experience the oneness He so desires to have with us.

And when you experience this oneness, when you allow yourself to adore His beautiful mouth for the healing, revelation, and authority that flow from it, you will begin to speak like Him. Your mouth will become like His mouth. You too will speak with authority. You too will expound upon revelation. You too will command healing to take place in the bodies of those who are sick.

HIS BEAUTIFUL LIPS

I can't close this chapter without mentioning the Lord's beautiful lips. This short, Biblical examination of His lips is, for obvious reasons, fitting.

From His beautiful lips proceed loving words that bring protection from the destroyer.

Concerning the works of men, by the word of thy lips I have kept me from the paths of the destroyer.
—Psalm 17:4 (KJV)

We also see a prophetically insightful psalm from King David regarding the grace-filled lips of Jesus.

Thou art fairer than the children of men: grace is poured into thy lips: therefore God hath blessed thee for ever.
—Psalm 45:2 (KJV)

From His lips also proceed peace and healing.

His cheeks are as a bed of spices, as sweet flowers: his lips like lilies, dropping sweet-smelling myrrh. Peace and healing come off his lips.
—Song of Solomon 5:13 (KJV)

In our times of purposeful adoration, let us not forget to make mention of the beautiful peace-giving lips of the Lord.

PURPOSEFUL ADORATION: HIS BEAUTIFUL MOUTH

Jesus, You are the only One with the true words of life. The truth and wisdom that come forth from Your beautiful mouth are all that sustain me. The entire world is held together based solely on what You spoke. I adore Your beautiful mouth and the voice it carries. I adore Your beautiful lips, which bring forth sweetness, healing, and peace. I worship Your smile, which shines Your grace and favor upon me. And as I worship Your beautiful mouth, let my mouth become like Yours. Speak through me as we become one—I in You, and You in me.

CHAPTER 7

HIS BEAUTIFUL BOSOM

In the bosom of Jesus, we find acceptance, security and riches. The Gospel of John begins and ends with narratives that make mention of the bosom.

No man hath seen God at any time; the only begotten Son, which is in the bosom of the Father, he hath declared him.
—John 1:18 (KJV)

Then Peter, turning about, seeth the disciple whom Jesus loved following; which also leaned on his breast at supper, and said, "Lord, which is he that betrayeth thee?"
—John 21:20 (KJV)

ACCEPTANCE

The bosom represents closeness. Jesus being "in the bosom of the Father" speaks of His consciousness perfectly dwelling within the heavenly Father. The Gospel of John opens with Christ being in the bosom of the Father, and closes with John being in the bosom of Christ. There is a replication taking place here. This indicates to us that after Christ completed His work, the intimacy Jesus had with the Father became the same intimacy you and I will share with Jesus. Christ is One with the Father, and now we are one with Christ.

The teaching on the acceptance we find in Jesus's bosom is inspired by the Joseph Prince sermon titled *"Know Him Whose Heart is to Serve You."*

This means that, through the bosom of Christ, we find a oneness, an acceptance, a divine embrace .

Toward the end of the book of John, he also mentions himself as "the disciple whom Jesus loved" and who "leaned on His breast at supper."

This speaks of a powerful revelation. We are made and called to live in the bosom of the Lord Jesus Christ, just like John the Beloved. John wasn't only conscious of his own love for Jesus; he was conscious of Jesus's love for him. He was so certain of Jesus's love for him that he gives himself the title of "the disciple whom Jesus loved." That's a bold confession of love.

We too are called to live in Jesus's consciousness about us. Know that you are loved by Jesus. Do as John did and call yourself His beloved. God is not a respecter of people. He wants all of us to think and speak like His beloved disciple John.

You should try it. Say out loud to yourself, "I am the one whom Jesus loves. I am His beloved."

The love of God intensely flows from the bosom of Jesus as an unstoppable force—a power that flows toward you. His love doesn't waver. The currents of His love are limitless and ever-strong, from moment to moment, day to day, and year to year. Surrender to His loving bosom. Lean on Him and find your peace of mind.

When John placed his head on the bosom of Jesus, he was filled with the peace of God that surpasses understanding.

The peace-filled love of Jesus flooded John's thoughts. He gives peace to our thought process, peace to our internal dialogue, and peace to our emotions. Jesus is the Prince of Peace, because He is able to inject His heavenly peace into every area of the mind.

By contrast, Peter was more conscious of his love for Jesus than he was of Jesus's love for him. Peter, in front of the other disciples, said that even if all the other disciples were to forsake Jesus, he never would.

Peter declared, "Even if everyone else deserts you, I will never desert you."
—Matthew 26:33 (NLT)

Yet, before the Crucifixion, despite his firm claims of loyalty, Peter forsook Jesus. We cannot count on our love for Jesus, because it fluctuates. Be like John who called himself the beloved, the disciple whom Jesus loved. Jesus loves you just as much as He loved John. Do you believe it? Are you aware of His love for you? Is your mind at peace in his bosom?

Lean in and find acceptance in His beautiful bosom.

SECURITY

He shall feed his flock like a shepherd: he shall gather the lambs with his arm, and carry them in his bosom, and shall gently lead those that are with young.
—Isaiah 40:11 (KJV)

Jesus's bosom represents His eternal role of Protector and Provider—even Servant. That He is willing to serve is one of the many reasons why you can be certain of your security in Him.

Jesus is the eternal One. The Son of God, Who created the entire universe and holds it together by His very existence, came to Planet Earth to serve His people. Jesus made that very clear by making this statement:

"For even the Son of Man came not to be served but to serve others and to give his life as a ransom for many."
—*Matthew 20:28 (NLT)*

Jesus portrayed this amazing servanthood and humility when He washed the feet of His disciples. But I want to point your attention to one specific thing He did while preparing to wash their feet: He laid aside His garments, took a towel, and girded Himself.

Jesus knowing that the Father had given all things into his hands, and that he was come from God, and went to God; He riseth from supper, and laid aside his garments; and took a towel, and girded himself.
—*John 13:3-4 (KJV)*

Jesus girded His bosom with a towel to serve, to wash the feet of His disciples, to cleanse them, and to show the world that He came to serve. It's amazing to think that Jesus, Who is the King of Heaven and earth, wants to serve His people and bless His Church.

Think about this: In John 13, Jesus girded Himself with a towel, but in Revelation 1, we see Him girded, not with a towel, but with a golden band around His bosom.

And standing in the middle of the lampstands was someone like the Son of Man. He was wearing a long robe with a gold sash across his chest.
—Revelation 1:13 (NLT)

Having once seen Jesus upon the earth, John, in the Book of Revelation, saw the glorified Jesus. But this time, Jesus was girded with a golden band. Jesus is girded as our King today to eternally serve His people. To save, heal, deliver, provide, and bless. He has not changed, and He will not change. Our Lord Jesus, Who rose from the dead and conquered every foe, wants to serve you and me. His beautiful bosom speaks of His love and serving nature. In that nature, we have our security. What an amazing Lord!

RICHES

When I turned to see who was speaking to me, I saw seven gold lampstands. And standing in the middle of the lampstands was someone like the Son of Man. He was wearing a long robe with a gold sash across his chest.
—Revelation 1:12-13 (NLT)

The Greek word for "sash" or "girdle" also translates as "purse," "money-carrying device," "belt," or "pocket." Across His bosom, the Lord has a golden sash. This, I believe, can represent abundance and riches.

When Jesus was commissioning His disciples into evangelistic outreach, He instructed them in this way:

"Heal the sick, raise the dead, cleanse the lepers, cast out demons. Freely you received, freely give. Do not acquire gold, or silver, or copper for your money belts."
—Matthew 10:8-9 (KJV)

When Jesus told His disciples not to acquire gold, silver, or copper in their money belts, He was teaching them to not rely upon themselves as their own source. In essence, He was saying, "Trust Me as your source. Lean on the riches and abundance stored in My bosom, wrapped in my golden sash."

We must understand that His golden girdle is overflowing with riches for us. The provision of Jesus comes through His girdle, through His bosom.

Blessed are those servants, whom the lord when he cometh shall find watching: verily I say unto you, that he shall gird himself, and make them to sit down to meat, and will come forth and serve them.
—Luke 12:37 (KJV)

Our gold, silver, copper, peace, joy, love, prosperity, and abundance are all found in the loving bosom of Jesus. Rest your head on His bosom and allow the riches of His golden girdle to fill your life with good things. He is our reward, and He is our source.

Purposeful Adoration:
His Beautiful Bosom

Beautiful Jesus, I accept Your invitation to rest my weary head on Your gracious and loving bosom, which is overflowing with acceptance and security. Master Jesus, I put my trust in the endless riches of Your golden sash as the source of provision for all the needs of my earthly life. Lord, I long to embrace the comforting warmth of Your beautiful bosom with all my heart.

CHAPTER 8

HIS BEAUTIFUL BACK

Now, of course, we know His beautiful back brings forth healing, for the Scripture makes that perfectly clear.

But he was wounded for our transgressions, he was bruised for our iniquities: the chastisement of our peace was upon him; and with his stripes we are healed.
—Isaiah 53:5 (KJV)

The Bible teaches us that His stripes, the whipping marks that He received on His beautiful back, bring forth healing. I could not write a chapter about the back of the Lord without at least mentioning the healing it brings. However, this thought is very commonly taught, so it's one I assume you already know. And since I already covered the topic of healing when writing of His hands, I want to teach now about an additional benefit of the Lord's back.

Did you know there is guidance to be found in His back? Believe it or not, it is a spiritual compass.

A COMPASS

I grew up in a godly home. My mom, dad, sister, grandmother, and cousins all lived together in one house. We were a big family, I know. While I have many typical childhood memories, I also remember how our home doubled as a church.

I don't mean we had regularly scheduled Sunday morning services complete with all the ministries you might find at a local church. I mean my parents would simply host worship and prayer gatherings. We would invite evangelists, prophets, and teachers into our home. My family is Assyrian; our culture emphasizes hospitality, but my parents are incredibly hospitable, even by Assyrian standards. So the ministers we invited to our meetings would stay in our home. We would even give up our beds to them at times. (Actually, it was mostly my grandmother who would do this. I rarely did so.)

We would invite people to join us for our meetings to hear the ministers, and people would flock to our home from all over the place. We would prepare feasts for them, barbecuing beef, chicken, and steak. Like I said: We were very hospitable.

To this day, I'm still impressed at how my parents and family demonstrated the love of God to people through their welcoming actions. The way they lived set a godly atmosphere in our home. We were always having Bible study meetings, people moving through, and spiritual experiences. Sometimes those meetings would last until three or four in the morning. Our home was busy with godly activity.

One week, we had a guest minister in our home who gave me a powerful prophetic word. Going into what seemed to be a spiritual vision, the minister faced me and said, "I see you, Dany, and I see the Lord Jesus. The Lord Jesus is standing on a path.

He's looking at you with loving eyes, and His eyes are calling you to follow Him. And the Lord Jesus has in His hand a book. This book—it's a golden book, and it's illuminated. There's a great light coming from the book. The Lord wants to give you this book. He wants you to follow Him. I see a long path in front of Him. I see you beginning to follow Him and walk along this path behind the Lord Jesus."

I was eighteen years old when that word was spoken over my life. It has stayed in my mind. I remember it clearly.

Looking back now, I know the path in the vision represented my life's journey, my calling, my ministry. That prophetic vision makes sense to me now, especially as it pertains to the area of purposeful adoration. Picture this: In that vision, when Jesus turned and began to lead me, His beautiful back was revealed. When Jesus reveals to us His back, He is leading us into the will of the Father.

When the Lord leads, His back becomes our guide, our compass. When we focus on the back of the Lord, we are being led into the heart of the Father. Jesus is in the Father, and if we will follow Him, we too can experience oneness with God.

"When I am raised to life again, you will know that I am in my Father, and you are in me, and I am in you."
—John 14:20 (NLT)

That's what Jesus was doing in that preacher's vision: He was leading me into oneness with God, into the perfect will of God.

To be honest with you, I can't remember that preacher's name, and I have no idea where he is today. But I remember that prophetic word. Still now, it stands out it my mind.

But note that in that vision, Jesus was carrying a golden book, which was to be handed over at a certain point along the journey. I truly believe the book Jesus carried is the one you're reading now. More importantly, it is the message of purposeful adoration, which has been given to me at this key juncture in my spiritual journey.

What an amazing thing it is when prophetic revelation comes full circle!

But this is bigger than a book, and He does not reveal His back just to me. He wants to reveal it to you, too. His back represents His leadership. His back represents His guidance. You can only catch the revelation of His back if you are following Him.

He calls to you now, beckoning you to join Him along the path of your journey into oneness with God. He says, "Come and follow me."

The Apostle Paul knew what it was to follow behind the Lord Jesus as I am describing.

"Be ye followers of me, even as I also am of Christ."
—1 Corinthians 11:1 (KJV)

When you focus on His back, you will begin to see the will of God. When you begin to see the will of God, you become like the Lord. The purposeful adoration of His back will bring about clarity regarding God's will.

Jesus said, "Follow me," and multitudes did. Thousands of people, spiritually speaking, looked at His back and walked after Him. When He said, "Follow me," He was metaphorically presenting His back as a "compass." Many who followed Him came to know the direction of God's ways. When we purposefully adore His back, when we worship the vertebrae and muscles and movements of His back, He gives us specific revelation for our lives.

Think about that! The tailor-made plans and purposes of God for your life are supernaturally revealed while you purposefully adore His back. When you worship the lordship of Jesus and ask Him for direction, have a notepad nearby so you can record what God shows you.

God has specific plans for each person's life, including yours. Just as no two fingerprints are the same, so no two paths are the same. His unique guidance is aimed at your unique being. So each one of us must personally have a revelation of the Lord's leadership. We must know the specific plans of God for our lives, but that only comes when we look at the "compass," the back of beautiful Jesus.

Leaders walk in front; followers are behind. Therefore, following Jesus requires you to position yourself where you can see His back. Walk behind Him and purposefully adore His back.

As you walk behind Him, the direction and purpose you seek will unfold before your eyes.

DIVINE DESTINY

God has predestined every single day of your life. When the Bible talks about predestination, it's not just talking about your salvation experience or having your name in the Book of Life. God has a predestined plan for every moment and for every day of your life. God has a perfect plan for your days, your moments, your experiences, and your relationships. Everything God has planned for your life has been written in His book of predestination. But the plans of God require your participation and obedience in order to see fulfillment.

So the question becomes, "What is preventing me from walking in the perfect, predestined plan of God for my life?" or "Why don't I experience the fullness of God's predestined plan daily?"

God moves through a linear series of events that culminate from a chain reaction of decisions. One simple, faith-filled act of obedience on your part can unlock a cluster of miracles.

Whenever you use the back of Jesus as your compass through adoration, Jesus will deposit supernaturally inspired thoughts in your mind. His tailor-made plans for your life will be made known. It's amazing how simple it really is to walk in God's perfect will. It's just a matter of revelation of and obedience to God's will. The revelation is found through the adoration of His beautiful back. The second part is a matter of your decisions.

When you worship the back of the Lord, which represents His lordship and leadership, you will be rewarded for your diligence.

But without faith it is impossible to please him: for he that cometh to God must believe that he is, and that he is a rewarder of them that diligently seek him.
—Hebrews 11:6 (KJV)

When you seek the guidance of the Lord, He is faithful to show you the way you should go. Sometimes, He will give you the idea to contact someone, to go somewhere, or to do something. These ideas can be very subtle, seemingly insignificant instructions that He will drop into your mind. Yet a small act of obedience will trigger a linear chain reaction of events that He has predestined for you to experience. But if we miss that initial window of instruction, it can pass by, and we will never know what was available to us. We must adore His beautiful back, receive revelation of His will, and then obey His leading. And we must obey His leading the very moment He provides it, or we will miss the entire process of events that should unfold as a result of that act of divinely appointed obedience.

The Lord has many linear, chain-reaction types of events ready to manifest before you every single day. It's not just one window of opportunity, but many, that appear before us throughout the day. And these many chain-reaction events all come together to become the predestined plan of God for your life. These plans have already been written by the Lord for your life.

You likely know what it's like to walk into a divinely appointed moment. Things just seem to click. It's a great spiritual sensation! The plans Jesus has already predetermined for your daily life manifest as you worship His back, if you acknowledge His lordship.

Then Jesus said to his disciples, "If any of you wants to be my follower, you must turn from your selfish ways, take up your cross, and follow me ..."
—*Matthew 16:24 (NLT)*

Pick up the cross and follow Him daily. Use His back as your compass. And when He deposits His thoughts and instructions into your mind, act! You will never know what that act will trigger unless you, by faith, choose to do it.

RADICAL FOLLOWERS

I must reiterate this, because I want you to really get it: There is one major stipulation to receiving the revelation of God's perfect will, the direction, and the guidance of Jesus's back. You must follow it.

Now the foundation of purposeful adoration is a combination of love and passionate obsession. Following Jesus is not something that can be done successfully out of mere discipline—though that is part of it. Instead, following Jesus must be done out of love.

To be a successfully radical follower of Christ, one must purposefully adore His back (His leadership and lordship).

In focusing on His back, in worshipping His back, we receive the needed fuel to carry out the spiritual journey.

So to follow Jesus simply means we focus our love upon Him through practicing the purposeful adoration of His back. And that specific adoration will always produce acts of obedience. We know the benefits of following His back. But to receive those benefits, we must join together with His mission, vision, and direction.

Jesus is constantly moving forward, and we are called to keep up with His movement, or we will begin to drift away from Him. Our love for His back keeps us close to His leadership; it keeps us following mere inches behind Him. His back is a key to union with Him. By practicing the purposeful adoration of His back, we are joining with Jesus our Lord, Who precedes us. We are siding with His company.

The back of Jesus is the door of invitation into the perfect will of God. His back is our compass. His back is the vehicle the Holy Spirit uses to guide us.

When Jesus invites us to follow Him, it's not because He is walking away from us and we are striving to keep up. On the contrary, He invites us to follow Him because He wants to lead us into His perfect plan for our lives, not leave us behind. He wants to show you what a supernatural life can look like on a daily basis. He wants to lead you to higher grounds of favor and deeper waters of wisdom.

But it takes someone radical in faith to follow Jesus. Following His back must come before anything else.

Another of his disciples said, "Lord, first let me return home and bury my father." But Jesus told him, "Follow me now. Let the spiritually dead bury their own dead."
—Matthew 8:21-22 (NLT)

It takes a truly obsessed Jesus lover to adore Him as specifically as purposeful adoration requires. To truly worship and adore His back requires that we drop all else. It requires us to fix our attention on Him. We cannot waver. We cannot compromise. We cannot let our vision be distracted by the alluring sights of this world. We must be stubborn in our decision to fix our eyes upon His back as He leads the way. Cling tightly to Him. Follow Him no matter the cost.

By choosing to follow Jesus above anyone or anything else, we are recognizing Him as being worthy of all our love and adoration. Jesus doesn't want to just have "first place" in our lives; He wants to have every place in our lives. He wants to fill every area with His overwhelming goodness and love. And through the overflow of His divine love we can then correctly love our families, neighbors, and friends. But adoring His back must come first. He is the leader; we are the followers. It's as simple as that!

He that loveth father or mother more than me is not worthy of me: and he that loveth son or daughter more than me is not worthy of me.
—Matthew 10:37 (KJV)

Don't be concerned with anything else, not even who is or isn't following Jesus as you are.

Peter turned around and saw behind them the disciple Jesus loved—the one who had leaned over to Jesus during supper and asked, "Lord, who will betray you?" Peter asked Jesus, "What about him, Lord?" Jesus replied, "If I want him to remain alive until I return, what is that to you? As for you, follow me." So the rumor spread among the community of believers that this disciple wouldn't die. But that isn't what Jesus said at all. He only said, "If I want him to remain alive until I return, what is that to you?"
—John 21:20-23 (KJV)

Stay focused, and look nowhere else but the back of Jesus. Be radical and purposefully adore and unconditionally follow His beautiful back.

BENEFITS OF ADORING HIS BACK

And as you commit to radically following Him through the purposeful adoration of His back, countless blessings will come your way. By no means do we follow the Lord for only the purpose of receiving His blessings, but we must not resist those blessings for the sake of false spirituality either.

When you follow the back of Jesus, angels follow you.

For he shall give his angels charge over thee, to keep thee in all thy ways.
—Psalm 91:11 (KJV)

When you follow the back of Jesus, goodness and mercy follow you.

Surely goodness and mercy shall follow me all the days of my life: and I will dwell in the house of the LORD for ever.
—Psalm 23:6 (KJV)

When you follow the back of Jesus, supernatural signs follow you.

"And these signs shall follow them that believe; In my name shall they cast out devils; they shall speak with new tongues; They shall take up serpents; and if they drink any deadly thing, it shall not hurt them; they shall lay hands on the sick, and they shall recover."
—Mark 16:17-18 (KJV)

Following after His back will cause others to follow Him through you. He made the disciples who chose to follow Him fishers of men. Those who dropped their nets and chose to follow Jesus themselves became great spiritual leaders.

Jesus called out to them, "Come, follow me, and I will show you how to fish for people!" And they left their nets at once and followed him.
—Matthew 4:19-20 (NLT)

Consider this too. God honors those who choose to follow His Son. He favors those who love His Son Jesus. God upholds those who follow after the back of Jesus.

"If any man serve me, let him follow me; and where I am, there shall also my servant be: if any man serve me, him will my Father honour."
—John 12:26 (KJV)

When you follow the back of Jesus, you walk in His divine light. Confusion, disillusionment, and demonic activity cannot coexist with the light of the world, our Lord Jesus.

"I am the light of the world: He that followeth Me shall not walk in darkness, but shall have the light of life."
—John 8:12 (KJV)

A final benefit I will mention—but which does not come close to completing the list of benefits that derive from adoring the beautiful back of Jesus—is that the presence of God will surround you in every way. Following Jesus's back will cause His presence to wrap all around you!

You hem me in behind and before, and you lay your hand upon me.
—Psalm 139:5 (KJV)

In the end, adoring the back of Jesus is all about an unconditional commitment to follow His lordship and leadership. The adoration of His back is the act of radical obedience based only on what the Lord has instructed. This sort of commitment, this self-abandoning faith, is rewarded with a progressive revelation of the perfect will of God.

Look at His back, His compass, today. Choose to follow Him.

Purposeful Adoration: His Beautiful Back

Beautiful Jesus, I commit again to a selfless following of Your lordship. With no conditions, I re-submit myself to you. I adore Your beautiful back, which is my source of direction. As I follow Your back along this spiritual journey, I ask You to keep me close. Let my love for You be my sustenance to continue in my obedience toward You. Thank You for Your back, which reveals Your will to me. Thank You for Your reliable and strong lordship. Thank You for Your beautiful back.

CHAPTER 9

HIS BEAUTIFUL ARMS

The arms of the Lord are mighty. In His arms, there is divine strength. Admiring the strength of the Lord, the psalmist David writes a praise-filled line of prophetic poetry:

Thou hast a mighty arm: strong is thy hand, and high is thy right hand.
—Psalm 89:13 (KJV)

And what is it the Lord does with such awesome and powerful strength? He pulls the lost and the bound into salvation and freedom. Only the arms of Jesus bring redemption and freedom from bondage.

Wherefore say unto the children of Israel, I am the LORD, and I will bring you out from under the burdens of the Egyptians, and I will rid you out of their bondage, and I will redeem you with a stretched out arm, and with great judgments ...
—Exodus 6:6 (KJV)

The outstretched arms of the Lord bring you great power and deliverance from every type of oppression. Nothing is a match for the strength in the arms of Jesus. Even the great and powerful pharaoh, ruler of Egypt, broke like a brittle leaf under the might of the Lord's arms.

But the LORD, who brought you up out of the land of Egypt with great power and a stretched out arm, him shall ye fear, and him shall ye worship, and to him shall ye do sacrifice.
—2 Kings 17:36 (KJV)

With His powerful arms, Jesus will fight your battles and bring help in your time of need.

With him is an arm of flesh; but with us is the LORD our God to help us, and to fight our battles. And the people rested themselves upon the words of Hezekiah king of Judah.
—2 Chronicles 32:8 (KJV)

Be encouraged! No situation you face is too difficult for the mighty arms of Jesus.

Ah Lord GOD! behold, thou hast made the heaven and the earth by thy great power and stretched out arm, and there is nothing too hard for thee.
—Jeremiah 32:17 (KJV)

Let the matter be settled. The holy arms of Jesus bring about marvelous victory—without exception.

O sing unto the LORD a new song; for he hath done marvellous things: his right hand, and his holy arm, hath gotten him the victory.
—Psalm 98:1 (KJV)

I can also describe how the Lord uses that same strength—which saves and delivers—to help us become established. This means He lends us His strength to make up for our weaknesses. The beautiful arms of Jesus will strengthen and establish every area of your life.

With whom my hand shall be established: mine arm also shall strengthen him.
—Psalm 89:21 (KJV)

Because of His strength, we share in His dominion, rewards, and blessings, which all come through His arms.

Behold, the Lord GOD will come with strong hand, and his arm shall rule for him: behold, his reward is with him, and his work before him.
—Isaiah 40:10 (KJV)

As capable as His arms are, they are, for you and me, perfect safety and impenetrable security. Truly, refuge is found in the loving arms of Christ. They provide salvation from harm.

My righteousness is near; my salvation is gone forth, and mine arms shall judge the people; the isles shall wait upon me, and on mine arm shall they trust.
—Isaiah 51:5 (KJV)

Digging further into the Scripture, we find Jesus referred to as "the arm of the Lord," because He is the will of God made manifest.

Who hath believed our report? and to whom is the arm of the LORD revealed? For he shall grow up before him as a tender plant, and as a root out of a dry ground: he hath no form nor comeliness; and when we shall see him, there is no beauty that we should desire him.
—*Isaiah 53:1-2 (KJV)*

That verse gives us a better idea of just how much strength is in His arm; it sufficed as a representation for His entire being. The arm of the Lord is miraculous through and through.

In fact, the glorious arms of the Lord can make a way for you when there seems to be no way forward.

That led them by the right hand of Moses with his glorious arm, dividing the water before them, to make himself an everlasting name?
—*Isaiah 63:12 (KJV)*

Again, I emphasize that nothing can stand before the strength of the Lord's arm. There is no situation stubborn enough to resist the will of God.

Furthermore, the powerful arms of Jesus, which made you and formed you, can also bless you.

With my great strength and powerful arm I made the earth and all its people and every animal. I can give these things of mine to anyone I choose.
—*Jeremiah 27:5 (NLT)*

The arms of the Lord bring promotion to the humble.

He hath shewed strength with his arm; he hath scattered the proud in the imagination of their hearts. He hath put down the mighty from their seats, and exalted them of low degree.
—Luke 1:51-52 (KJV)

Now consider this eye-opening thought: The arms of the Lord endured great pain for you.

The beautiful arms of Jesus were stretched out and tied to the cross of Calvary in order to pay the ultimate price for our redemption and wholeness. Jesus voluntarily gave His beautiful arms to be bound with ropes, and He was led to the cross so we could walk in complete liberty in every area of life.

And straightway in the morning the chief priests held a consultation with the elders and scribes and the whole council, and bound Jesus, and carried him away, and delivered him to Pilate.
—Mark 15:1 (KJV)

PURPOSEFUL ADORATION:
HIS BEAUTIFUL ARMS

Lord Jesus, I adore Your powerful arms, which are mighty to save. Thank You for stretching out Your arms upon the cruel cross to deliver me from every foe. I honor Your beautiful arms, which bring strength to my weak areas, establish my life in Your blessings, and pave the way for me in every difficult situation. I praise You Lord, for Your protective, gentle and loving arms.

CHAPTER 10

HIS BEAUTIFUL HANDS

Consider the blessed hands of Christ. They were the tools of the Father that brought about dramatic transformation in the lives of all who were graced with a touch. His hands were powerful enough to heal, personal enough to touch, humble enough to master carpentry, and loving enough to be violently marked by sin-driven nails.

With His hands, He gives needed sustenance, and with those same hands, He receives you as His own. His hands give life, and they take away pain. Yes, consider the blessed hands of beautiful Jesus Christ!

What do they hold? What do they sustain? What do they give?

I want to draw your attention to a famous Bible story in which Jesus cleanses a desperate leper.

In one of the villages, Jesus met a man with an advanced case of leprosy. When the man saw Jesus, he bowed with his face to the ground, begging to be healed. "Lord," he said, "if you are willing, you can heal me and make me clean." Jesus reached out and touched him. "I am willing," he said. "Be healed!" And instantly the leprosy disappeared.
—Luke 5:12-13 (NLT)

Leprosy is an irritating and embarrassing skin infection that—though treatable now with drugs—often led to deformities and even the loss of body parts in Jesus's day. Those who were unfortunate enough to be plagued by this infectious and stigmatizing disease were labeled as "unclean"; they were forced to live in colonies on the outskirts of town, where the disease could not be spread to others. They were cast out of the community, away from their families and loved ones. Leprosy was not only a disfiguring disease to have back then, but an extremely lonely one.

And the priest shall look on the plague in the skin of the flesh: and when the hair in the plague is turned white, and the plague in sight be deeper than the skin of his flesh, it is a plague of leprosy: and the priest shall look on him, and pronounce him unclean.
—Leviticus 13:3 (KJV)

Or suppose you unknowingly touch something that makes a person unclean. When you realize what you have done, you must admit your guilt.
—Leviticus 5:3 (NLT)

But the leper in Luke 5 would escape the shame of such a label. He found himself within Christ's range of touch. Seeing Jesus, the leper buried his face into the ground. Humbly he begged for the cleansing touch of Jesus. "Lord," he pleaded, "if you are willing, you can heal me and make me clean." If only he understood Jesus's power and heart, he would not have begged in such a way.

Jesus assured the ailed man, "I am willing." And then Christ commanded, "Be healed!" Matthew's account of this story gives us a powerful detail that Luke omitted:

Jesus reached out and touched him. "I am willing," he said. "Be healed!"
And instantly the leprosy disappeared.
—*Matthew 8:3 (NLT)*

Jesus touched the leper. Jesus touched the unclean thing. He, in His loving compassion, took upon the label of being unclean Himself.

That's what the cleansing touch of Jesus does. It takes the filth and gives cleansing. Jesus took the man's disease, as well as his shame. The leprosy of the leper was cleansed when Jesus touched him.

Analogously speaking, leprosy can be symbolic for sin. With one touch, the hands of Jesus can cleanse any and all unclean things from your life. His hands can remove the filth of sin. Jesus even wants to reach into the areas of secret sin, areas that remain hidden from others, and bring cleansing. Jesus is the only One Who can reach into that area of your life. He's the only One Who can touch you and heal you of hidden bondage that steals your joy.

His beautiful hands bring cleansing.

The hands of Jesus also carry the cure to any sickness or disease. His hands bring divine healing. His beautiful nail-scarred hands are forever stretched out toward a world that is full of illness and pestilence. They are ready to heal at any moment.

Looking again to the portion of Scripture that we just examined, I want you to note the statement of the leper. He cried, "Lord, if you are willing …"

"… if you are willing …"

Is it God's will to heal?

Jesus responds to this question. Without hesitation, He told the leper, "I am willing. Be healed!" And His answer has not changed.

Jesus Christ the same yesterday, and today, and forever.
—Hebrews 13:8 (KJV)

In fact, today the Lord's reach goes even further than when He walked the earth, because He now sits on Heaven's throne with all dominion and authority as the glorified and resurrected King.

Therefore, God elevated him to the place of highest honor and gave him the name above all other names …
—Philippians 2:9 (NLT)

So the question isn't really "Can Jesus heal?" or "Is Jesus willing to heal?"

The answer to both questions is a resounding "yes"! The correct question should be, "How do I receive His healing touch upon my mind and body?"

Here's one example: My family and I experienced the healing touch of beautiful Jesus when we needed it most.

ABIGAIL'S HEALING

On August 24, 2012, my first child, Abigail, was born. Abigail's delivery was long and difficult. When she finally was born, the doctors informed us of complications with her development. Apparently, she had not been feeding properly on the placenta, and was therefore born underweight, at just under five pounds.

So the doctors whisked her away to perform a blood sugar analysis and check for other irregularities. It turned out her blood sugar was incredibly low. Obviously, we were very concerned. That's a given.

A few minutes later, they checked Abigail's blood sugar again, and found it was even worse, having dropped to a dangerously low level. That is a very serious complication, especially for a newborn baby, and Abigail was rushed to the hospital's neonatal intensive care unit.

We were unable to hold our baby or otherwise experience the precious first moments parents typically do after a normal delivery.

The doctors assured us the complications, though not ideal, were relatively common and fixable with a few days of intravenous feeding and constant monitoring. So the medical team attached an IV, along with some monitoring equipment, to Abigail's left arm. They monitored her for hours, re-inserting the IV every so often. Eventually, they ran out of veins on Abigail's left arm to use, so they switched to her right arm. When they ran out of veins there, they began using the veins in her forehead.

After a day and a half, I began to worry, because the numbers had not yet stabilized. They remained extremely low, making it impossible to remove her from the IV. This complication with my daughter's blood was a stubborn one.

Before Abigail's birth, I did not know what it was to love my own child. Now, I had been blessed with an indescribable and newfound love, but it came with a level of concern I had never known before, either. Truly, the whole situation was becoming difficult to bear. We were a young family, I was a young man, and Abigail was a young baby. And there I was, helplessly watching my firstborn, my little infant daughter. She had tubes everywhere. It was awful.

About two days into the complications, a member of the medical staff approached me and explained, "We're running out of veins. We need to run a line into a main artery in one of your daughter's legs." Upon hearing those matter-of-fact words, I cringed. It almost physically hurt me to think of it.

As much as I hated the thought of that procedure, I knew something had to be done. Deep within me, I hoped that would be the worst of it. I hoped it would be a turning point. I prayed for Abigail's numbers to normalize.

A short while later, we were approached by yet another member of the medical staff, who gave us more bad news.

"Abigail may have a tumor on her pancreas that's secreting insulin," he said.

I froze. Waves of worry and sadness rushed over me as he continued, "There's also a bump on the side of her head. We need to proceed with a CT scan."

I was numb. And he kept speaking, finishing by saying:

"Your daughter may be on medication for the rest of her life."

As the news continued to pummel my mind and emotions, I felt as if I weren't in that moment. Something was said about needing to fly Abigail to a children's hospital in Philadelphia and the possibility that she might not recover. As those words hovered in the air around me, I began to pray internally.

I went home, lay on the floor, and cried. Deep and uncontrollable sobs stole my breath. I was deeply anguished. Images of Abigail flashed before my mind—her little body surrounded by medical equipment, her tiny limbs riddled with needle holes. She was so helpless. I felt helpless.

With my fist pounding the ground where I lay, I cried out to the Lord.

"Jesus," I prayed, "I've seen You do miracles all around the world! I've watched Your power in action. You heal people at my services! Now, look at what I'm going through. I need You!"

I don't remember when exactly, but eventually I drifted into sleep.

The next day, I awoke. Looking back on that moment, I am reminded of the Scripture that says,

Weeping may last through the night, but joy comes with the morning.
—Psalm 30:5 (NLT)

In that moment, His joy became my strength. The Lord truly strengthened me. I could feel it.

I grabbed my Bible, left the house, and headed to the hospital. I had a fresh faith and a hopeful determination. I began to call all my fellow prayer warriors and enlisted them to back me in faith-filled prayers.

I walked into the room where they were monitoring my Abigail, my heart full of expectation. I placed my phone beside my daughter and played anointed worship music. The atmosphere of that room began to change. I proceeded to read healing Scriptures aloud; I spoke them as declarations over Abigail. I boldly proclaimed, "All is well. You shall be healed."

Around this time, the medical team was making a shift change. One of the staff members came into the room to update me with more negative news. At that point, however, I was only interested in what the Word of God said concerning Abigail's situation.

I must point out here that I am not against the practice of medicine or medical expertise. I don't believe in living in denial. But there are moments when we need to just focus on the Word of God. This, of course, does not mean we should consistently ignore medical advice; I just mean all things must be heard and considered in their proper context. God is not limited by our understanding, our circumstances, or our methods.

That poor staff member had no idea what he'd just stepped into. I looked him straight in the eye and said, "You know something, sir? The Lord Jesus Christ—the God of Abraham, Isaac, and Jacob—is going to touch my daughter. And you're going to see it with your eyes."

A little taken aback, he said, "I'll take all the help I can get."

That evening, I sought the Lord. My prayers were non-stop offered to God until I was drained. Nevertheless, I culminated my time of prayer with communion.

After taking communion, Jesus appeared to me in that hospital room. I saw Him stand before me. And when I saw Him, I knew in my heart He was going to touch my Abigail. I knew all was going to be well.

But even after catching a glimpse of beautiful Jesus, I continued to pray deep into the night. After hours of persistent prayer, we finally went home. And I knew that I knew Jesus had done something for Abigail.

When the morning came, we went back to the hospital. Something was different in the atmosphere. The spiritual struggle was not there. There was a peace, a calm in the spirit. We waited to hear an update. Eventually, a staff member approached us.

"Good news," he said. "We got the results from your daughter's CT scan. We didn't find anything in her pancreas. And that bump on her head that we found during the sonogram? It's gone."

Over the next two days, Abigail's blood normalized. We took her home three days after the Lord appeared to me in the hospital.

As I write this now, Abigail is four years old. She's beautiful, has green eyes, and is very bright. She's witty, funny, intellectual, spiritual, and perceptive. She is beyond what I could have dreamed to have in a daughter. She's living up to her name, which means "her father's rejoicing." She is her father's joy.

She is a living testimony of the healing touch of Jesus.

So how do we receive His healing touch?

We receive it in the same way we receive anything from the Lord, any promise from His sure Word: By faith.

Today, right now, if you reach out by faith to His healing hands, you can receive from Him. If God did it for that leper, He will do it for you. If He's healed others, it means He will heal you. How do I know this? Simple. The Bible says,

For God does not show favoritism.
—Romans 2:11 (NLT)

If, while living upon the earth in a physical body, Jesus healed everyone who came to Him, He will do the same for you today.

His hands bring healing.

Reflecting just upon the cleansing and healing nature of His hands, we are awed and driven to gratitude. However, there is more. For the Lord's hands don't just bring cleansing, though that in and of itself is a wonderful gift. His hands aren't limited to healing, though we thank Him continually for His healing power. Amazingly, the Lord's hands also have resurrection life in them. He has the very touch of life.

In the Gospel of Luke, we are told an inspiring story that powerfully illustrates Christ's life-giving touch.

Soon afterwards He went to a city called Nain; and His disciples were going along with Him, accompanied by a large crowd. Now as He approached the gate of the city, a dead man was being carried out, the only son of his mother, and she was a widow; and a sizeable crowd from the city was with her.

When the Lord saw her, He felt compassion for her, and said to her, "Do not weep." And He came up and touched the coffin; and the bearers came to a halt. And He said, "Young man, I say to you, arise!" The dead man sat up and began to speak. And Jesus gave him back to his mother.
—Luke 7:11-15 (NLT)

Put yourself in the widow's place. Empathize. Imagine. Picture.

You're on your way to lay your loved one's body to rest. A grieving procession escorts you. You feel the pain of loss, and the harsh reality—the sight of your loved one's casket—is more than you feel you can stand.

Suddenly, Jesus walks up to you, tells you not to weep, and touches the casket. To your shock and joy—and perhaps a little to your horror—your loved one sits up and begins to speak.

Can you imagine the fear and the joy? Can you hear the reaction of the people in the funeral procession?

The family who was there to mourn found unexpected joy. They went from dread to jubilance, from crying tears of grief to crying tears of laughter and joy. They went from playing funeral music to a song of celebration! What a difference the touch of Jesus can make! In one instant, everything can change in your favor. It only takes a single touch from the beautiful hands of Jesus.

Jesus raised that widow's son to life by simply touching the casket. With just a touch, the Lord can bring life to every dead area of your life. He can resurrect your dormant dreams and empower them all the way to beautiful fulfillment. The son of that poor widow had died prematurely, just like you may think certain dreams have died prematurely. But one touch of His hand can bring anything back to life.

His hands bring life.

Indeed, the Lord's hands are beautiful. I marvel at the truth that there's more to His touch than we can fully appreciate. For not only is there cleansing, healing, and life in His hands, there is also prosperity.

MORE THAN ENOUGH

The Lord challenged His disciples' faith, instructing them to feed a hungry multitude. The disciples thought with the natural mind and allowed lack to dethrone their faith.

Jesus soon saw a huge crowd of people coming to look for him. Turning to Philip, he asked, "Where can we buy bread to feed all these people?" He was testing Philip, for he already knew what he was going to do. Philip replied, "Even if we worked for months, we wouldn't have enough money to feed them!" Then Andrew, Simon Peter's brother, spoke up. "There's a young boy here with five barley loaves and two fish. But what good is that with this huge crowd?"

"Tell everyone to sit down," Jesus said. So they all sat down on the grassy slopes. (The men alone numbered about 5,000.) Then Jesus took the loaves, gave thanks to God, and distributed them to the people. Afterward he did the same with the fish. And they all ate as much as they wanted. After everyone was full, Jesus told his disciples, "Now gather the leftovers, so that nothing is wasted." So they picked up the pieces and filled twelve baskets with scraps left by the people who had eaten from the five barley loaves.
—*John 6:5-13 (NLT)*

What was lack for men became abundance at Jesus's touch. He took what wasn't enough and turned it into more than enough.

Are you living in lack today? Is what you have not enough to make it through the month? Are you struggling from paycheck to paycheck? Are you longing for freedom from the frustration of lack?

The answer is in Him.

The blessing of the LORD makes a person rich, and he adds no sorrow with it.
—*Proverbs 10:22 (NLT)*

Truly, there is prosperity in His hands.

What else is in His hands? You are!

Yes, you are in His hands.

And I give unto them eternal life; and they shall never perish, neither shall any man pluck them out of my hand.
—John 10:28 (KJV)

We are eternally secure from demonic powers, from sickness, and from death. No man can snatch us from His loving grip. You are forever His. The hands that were scarred to rescue you are the same that refuse to lose you.

In fact, everyone who has ever confessed Jesus as Lord is in His eternally secure grip. The Church in is His hands.

He held seven stars in his right hand, and a sharp two-edged sword came from his mouth. And his face was like the sun in all its brilliance.
—Revelation 1:16 (NLT)

The seven stars are the seven churches of Revelation. In other words, they represent the Church. He firmly grasps all who belong to Him within His mighty hands.

What's more? The final judgment is in His hands, in His sovereign control.

"I am the living one. I died, but look—I am alive forever and ever! And I hold the keys of death and the grave."
—Revelation 1:18 (NLT)

Your fate is in His hands. The final pronouncement is in His hands. All that you need is in His beautiful hands.

His Fingers

As a side note on the topic of the Lord's beautiful hands, I want to direct your attention to a few pivotal functions of the fingers of the Lord.

Jesus's fingers were active in the work of creation, and they can bring the same creative power into your life today.

When I consider thy heavens, the work of thy fingers, the moon and the stars, which thou hast ordained.
—Psalm 8:3 (KJV)

The fingers of Jesus carry the power to deliver you from any demonic spirit that opposes you.

But if I with the finger of God cast out devils, no doubt the kingdom of God has come upon you.
—Luke 11:20

With His beautiful finger, Jesus stooped down in the temple and wrote the law of grace on the ground, acquitting and forgiving the woman caught in the act of adultery.

This they said, tempting him, that they might have to accuse him. But Jesus stooped down, and with his finger wrote on the ground, as though he heard them not.
—John 8:6 (KJV)

It doesn't take much from Jesus to change your life forever—just a simple touch.

PURPOSEFUL ADORATION:
HIS BEAUTIFUL HANDS

Jesus, I stretch my hands toward Your beautiful hands. Please reach out and touch me. I need Your cleansing, healing, prospering, sovereign touch. I reach out to You in faith, and I ask You to connect with me. Touch me, Lord. Touch me, and I will be made whole. Touch me, and I will lack nothing. Thank You for what I am now receiving from Your hands. I adore Your hands. I kiss them in the spirit. I honor them with all my heart. Thank You, Jesus, for Your beautiful hands.

CHAPTER 11

HIS BEAUTIFUL LEGS

One of the basic functions of our legs is to provide us the ability to walk. Therefore, when we talk about the powerful legs of the Lord, I want you to think about the Son of God walking intimately with you. The supernatural legs of Jesus give Him the ability to walk with us in uninterrupted intimacy. He walks beside us every day, blessing us with HIs beautiful presence.

The walking legs of the Lord produce the sound of intimacy. Adam and Eve heard that joyful sound in the Garden of Eden every day—until the Fall.

And they heard the sound of the LORD God walking in the garden in the cool of the day, and Adam and his wife hid themselves from the presence of the LORD God among the trees of the garden.
—Genesis 3:8 (NKJV)

Adam and Eve hid themselves in shame and fear because they had chosen to forfeit the privilege of walking with the Lord by partaking of the forbidden tree in the garden. Today, we are living under a new and better covenant that completely hinges on the unmerited favor of Jesus and not our works. Therefore, we can walk without shame or fear because Christ has forever perfected us through the finished work of the cross and He has promised to never take away the joyful sound of His walking legs from our lives.

Let your conduct be without covetousness; be content with such things as you have. For He Himself has said, "I will never leave you nor forsake you."
—Hebrews 13:5 (NKJV)

The legs of the Lord walking intimately beside us bring many supernatural benefits to our lives. I would like to list a few of those benefits.

Intimately walking with Jesus will keep you prepared for the unknowable moment of the Rapture. Enoch was suddenly taken away as the walking legs of the Lord moved beside him every day.

And Enoch walked with God; and he was not, for God took him.
—Genesis 5:24 (NKJV)

Noah was called "perfect in his generation" because He walked with the perfect Savior. The moving legs of the Lord walking beside you will establish you on the just path of His perfect righteousness.

This is the genealogy of Noah. Noah was a just man, perfect in his generations. Noah walked with God.
—Genesis 6:9 (NKJV)

The legs of the Lord moving with you will keep you safe from the destructive plans of the enemy.

The fiery furnace was designed by the enemy to destroy the three Hebrew boys, but the fire could not hurt them because they intimately walked with the Son of God. His mighty legs will cause you to have victory over any cataclysmic situation!

"Look!" he answered, "I see four men loose, walking in the midst of the fire; and they are not hurt, and the form of the fourth is like the Son of God."
—Daniel 3:25 (NKJV)

The power unleashed through of legs of the Lord will allow you to supernaturally walk over the impossibilities of life. Peter was empowered to walk on top of the water as though it was dry land.

So He said, "Come." And when Peter had come down out of the boat, he walked on the water to go to Jesus.
—Matthew 14:29 (NKJV)

The movement produced by the legs of Jesus walking toward us will always reveal Him as the Lamb that was slain to take away the sins of the world.

And looking at Jesus as He walked, he said, "Behold the Lamb of God!"
—John 1:36 (NKJV)

Lastly, as the beautiful body of Jesus lifelessly hung on the cross, God did not allow the Roman soldiers to break the legs of His Son, thus fulfilling the Old Testament prophecy that "not one of His bones shall be broken."

This is significant because it declares to us the surety of our salvation. Though He bore our sin in His body, sin could not break the unshakeable pillar of His legs, which eternally uphold the purchased redemption of our glorified Lord.

But when they came to Jesus and saw that He was already dead, they did not break His legs.
—John 19:33 (NKJV)

PURPOSEFUL ADORATION:
HIS BEAUTIFUL LEGS

Precious Jesus, I love the joy-filled sound of intimacy that Your walking legs produce in my life. I give You praise for the many benefits that Your legs impart to me; preparation for the Rapture, establishment on the path of righteousness, victory over every attack, and power over the impossibilities of life. Lord Jesus, I honor Your powerful legs, which are the unshakeable pillars of my eternal salvation.

CHAPTER 12

HIS BEAUTIFUL FEET

When I was in my early twenties, the Lord was visiting me in a beautiful and special way, and I was getting to know Him intimately. During that time, a man about my age came to me asking for prayer.

So I joined him and another individual in a quiet room in the corner of a church. We all got on our knees to form a prayer circle, and each took turns calling upon Jesus.

At this time, I had really begun to develop a profound love for the Person of Jesus. That love had manifested itself as an untamable yearning to see the Lord more clearly, to know Him more intimately. And as I was keeling there in the prayer circle, my face just a few inches off the ground, my eyes tightly closed, I saw, in the spirit, the feet of Jesus appear right before my face.

The first thing I noticed were the nail scars in His feet. There was also a beautiful, luminous bronze glow around them that caught my attention. Yes, my eyes were closed, but the spiritual realm is more real than the natural realm. So this vision was as intense as anything you might experience in the natural—actually more so.

This was one of the first times I participated in purposeful adoration. And I had no idea what I was doing. It just came naturally—or more appropriately, supernaturally.

I didn't know the benefits or the importance of purposeful adoration. I had yet to even coin the term. But there I was, seeing the feet of Jesus in the spirit and purposefully adoring Him.

The words that came out of my mouth were inspired by the Holy Spirit. I started to say things to the Lord about His feet. I worshipped: "Thank You for Your feet. I thank You that Your feet appeared here. I thank You that You are here. I thank You for these nails scars. I love these nail scars. I'm so appreciative of them. I'm so thankful for what You've done for me. I just love You!"

So I began to purposefully, specifically, pour worship upon His feet. I described what His feet had accomplished and what they meant to me. I spoke of the accomplishments of His beautiful feet, of the nail scars, of the crushing victory over Satan's head, of the position of His feet's victorious stance on the footstool of Heaven, and so forth.

Little did I know the Lord would use that unique experience as a catalyst for this book.

If we are to focus on the Lord's beautiful feet, we must posture ourselves with low and humble reverence. Spiritually speaking, the lower you bow, the closer you are to His beautiful feet. You cannot fully appreciate His feet from afar. The closer you are, the more detailed they become. In the spirit, we fall at the feet of Jesus through humility, repentance, love, and the God-centered act of worship.

And she had a sister called Mary, which also sat at Jesus's feet, and heard his word.
—*Luke 10:39 (KJV)*

Is that not the true heart of worship? Certainly we can express our worship in song and in word. But Mary heard the Lord's Word. Hearing and obeying the Word of God is the ultimate act of humility and worship. At His feet we, like Mary, must also hear His Word. That is ultimate posture of worship.

Mary received divine revelation because she sat at Jesus's feet to hear His words. Jesus is the Word of God (John 1:1). Therefore, we must sit at His feet bowed in a position of worship. That nearness to Him best positions us to hear His words. Worshipping His feet prepares our hearts to receive the Word.

The lowliness that places us at the feet of Jesus is something we must regularly and frequently allow in our lives. The grasping of Jesus's feet is paralleled with worship. When we focus our worship upon His feet, Jesus focuses His attention upon our requests.

And as they went, Jesus met them and greeted them. And they ran to him, grasped his feet, and worshiped him.
—*Matthew 28:9 (NLT)*

We too must become so desperate for the Lord and His direction that we posture our hearts at the Master's feet. As we worship at the Lord's feet and hear His Word, we become prepared to follow in His steps.

Then Jesus said to his disciples, "If any of you wants to be my follower, you must turn from your selfish ways, take up your cross, and follow me."
—Matthew 16:24

Worshipping at the Lord's feet isn't limited to humble adoration; it matures into bold steps of faith taken behind the Lord. If we truly want to appreciate His nail-pierced feet, then we must take steps of obedience. We must leave the familiarity of comfort and go bravely into the risky ventures that require faith.

Be assured that we can trust the Lord. The feet we follow are the ones under which all things have been divinely placed. When you follow the feet of the Lord in obedience, the opposition you face today will crumble.

For Christ must reign until he humbles all his enemies beneath his feet. And the last enemy to be destroyed is death. For the Scriptures say, "God has put all things under his authority."
—1 Corinthians 15:25-27

When we sit at His feet in worship, we are doing the one thing that is needed, and we are positioning ourselves under His authority. Then we become delegates of His authority. When we follow in Christ's steps, we step where He steps, and we step over what He steps over.

Every enemy under His feet is under your feet when you walk in sync with the Lord. When you step in Christ's steps, you cannot walk in a curse; you can only walk in blessing.

In every place the enemy tries to hold in your life, you have the authority to stomp Him out. There is no safer place to step than in the path of the Lord's feet.

The Lord's authority is so absolute that He even stepped over the very laws of physics. Nature itself yields to the commanding steps of the Lord. The waters reverently stood at attention to escort the Authority of authorities.

Meanwhile, the disciples were in trouble far away from land, for a strong wind had risen, and they were fighting heavy waves. About three o'clock in the morning Jesus came toward them, walking on the water. When the disciples saw him walking on the water, they were terrified. In their fear, they cried out, "It's a ghost!" But Jesus spoke to them at once. "Don't be afraid," he said. "Take courage. I am here!"
—Matthew 14:24-27

When we follow Jesus, honoring the steps of His feet, we inevitably will step into the supernatural realm. When you worship Him in this way, your steps are marked by miracles.

Purposeful Adoration:
His Beautiful Feet

Jesus, I humbly bow myself before Your beautiful feet. Here, in my posture of humility, I can see Your feet more clearly. Thank You, Jesus, for Your lovely feet that crushed the head of Satan. I worship those feet that walked out of the tomb in Jerusalem and ascended into Heaven for me. I love those feet, which are victoriously positioned on Heaven's footstool. I thank You for Your beautiful feet, under which all things have been finally placed. I worship Your beautiful feet that stand grounded in divine authority. I want to follow Your feet no matter where they step, for they are beautiful. Thank You, Lord, for Your beautiful feet

CHAPTER 13

His Beautiful Features

Besides what can be called the "primary features" of the Lord, there are multiple other features that deserve to be mentioned. Because they don't each necessarily require an entire chapter to unfold, I have decided to place them here in a chapter that covers them all.

In this chapter, I want to write to you about the following features of the Lord:

• His shoulders;
• His forehead; and
• His organs.

His Beautiful Shoulders

The majestic shoulders of Jesus carry the governmental authority of His kingdom. When we focus our love upon the shoulders of the Lord through the act of purposeful adoration, He releases the power and authority of His heavenly Kingdom in our lives.

For unto us a Child is born, unto us a Son is given and the government shall be upon His shoulder, and His name shall be called Wonderful, Counsellor, the mighty God, the Everlasting Father, the Prince of Peace.
—Isaiah 9:8 (KJV)

The shoulders of Jesus will also give you the power to successfully carry your cross and turn from your selfish ways.

Then Jesus said to His disciple, "If any of you wants to be My follower, you must turn from your selfish ways, take up your cross and follow Me."
—Matthew 16:24 (NLT)

His Beautiful Forehead

The beautiful forehead of Jesus blesses the path upon which you walk and breaks every curse in your life. When facing the pressures of the cross before Him, Jesus began to sweat drops of blood from His forehead onto the ground.

He prayed more fervently, and he was in such agony of spirit that his sweat fell to the ground like great drops of blood.
—Luke 22:44 (NLT)

The Book of Genesis tells us the ground is cursed.

And to the man he said, "Since you listened to your wife and ate from the tree whose fruit I commanded you not to eat, the ground is cursed because of you. All your life you will struggle to scratch a living from it."
—Genesis 3:17 (NLT)

Since the curse of sin came upon the ground, man has lived by toil and stress. Before Christ, man was under the curse.

In Eden, the first garden, a curse came upon the ground, but in Gethsemane, the second garden, the blood Jesus sweat from His forehead broke that curse. Only under extreme pressure can the capillaries burst, causing you to sweat blood. This means Jesus was agonized in order to bless you and reverse any curse upon your life.

Jesus's saving, redeeming blood fell upon a cursed ground, redeeming us from it. The curse of stress and toil has been broken through His beautiful forehead. His blood fell to the ground before Him; therefore, the blood of His forehead goes before you. Everywhere you go, in every room you enter, you have the precious blood of Jesus going before you and setting you up for favor and protection. Be happy, be joyful, and be at peace, because the forehead of your Master has blessed your going in and your coming out.

Consider the fact that the curse of the garden also brought poverty. You see, before the curse of sin, vegetation and plant life grew without inhibition. However, after sin destroyed the world, thorns grew and choked the fruitfulness of the once-perfect ground. Not only did Jesus bleed upon the ground to bless your path and break curses, but He also bled upon the thorns—those useless thorns that choke out prosperity—to break the power of poverty. Thorns prevent fruitfulness, but the blood from Jesus's forehead touched them, too.

The soldiers wove a crown of thorns and put it on his head, and they put a purple robe on him.
—John 19:2 (NLT)

Thorns and thistles were part of the curse of poverty. Think how hard one must toil to make a living from the ground. But thank God that Jesus's forehead bled upon the thorns! As the crown of thorns was slowly forced into His skin, the curse of poverty was broken. The thorns troubled Jesus, so they have no right to trouble you.

Your path is blessed. Your curses are broken. Your prosperity is assured. That's all thanks to the beautiful forehead of Jesus.

His Beautiful Organs

In the twelfth chapter of Exodus, God instructed the children of Israel to choose a spotless lamb and cook it with fire. That symbolized Christ's suffering at the cross. The Lord further instructed the Israelites to eat the lamb's entrails. We too must partake of the inner person of the Lord Jesus, the perfect Lamb of God. We must even give worship to His internal organs, because they are the most perfect internal organs of any human ever to have lived.

Now think about this: As He is, so are we to be. As we worship Him, His perfection can and must be imparted to us in the form of divine health. If you have a kidney problem, worship His perfect kidneys.

The same principle can be applied to any of His body parts, really. If you have a back problem, worship His perfected back. Worship His organs and bones and muscles.

Whatever needs to become whole in you, worship the same part of the Lord's body. Focus on the Lord Jesus, because He is health and life. As He is, so are we now.

Let's go back to the Old Testament to look again at the shadow of Christ. When God gave His Passover instructions to the children of Israel, He told them to roast and partake of the whole lamb—even the internal organs.

Do not eat any of the meat raw or boiled in water. The whole animal— including the head, legs, and internal organs—must be roasted over a fire. —Exodus 12:9 (NLT)

Every part of our Lord Jesus is divine and perfect, including His internal organs. In Exodus, I believe God is painting a very detailed picture for us about His Son Jesus. That picture is now revealing the fact that every part of Jesus is available to us that we might walk in His wholeness. His body is available for us to partake of—even His perfectly functioning, eternal, internal organs.

For my flesh is true food, and my blood is true drink. —John 6:55 (NLT)

Today, if you need healing or a touch from God in your inner parts, look to Jesus and praise Him for His perfect internal organs. Partake of Him through communion and worship. Praise and worship every part of the Lord and receive from His abundance. Remember:

As Jesus is, so are we in this world, now. His organs and inner parts are perfect, and Jesus is ready to impart that perfection to you.

Herein is our love made perfect, that we may have boldness in the day of judgment: because as he is, so are we in this world.
—1 John 4:17 (KJV)

The same applies to His rarely thought-of nervous system, lymphatic system, skeleton, and so forth.

PURPOSEFUL ADORATION: HIS BEAUTIFUL FEATURES

Beautiful Jesus, I thank You for Your rarely mentioned features. I want to adore and praise You for every detail of Who You are. Thank You for Your shoulders, forehead, and even Your internal organs. Thank You for the authority set upon me through Your shoulders, the blessing that graces me through Your forehead, and the wholeness I receive from Your every part—including your organs. Thank You, precious Jesus, that as You are, so am I. Help me to never take for granted any part of You.

CHAPTER 14

HIS BEAUTIFUL BLOOD

The beautiful blood of Jesus carries the genetic code of Almighty God. And we have been purchased by that flawless blood.

Therefore take heed to yourselves and to all the flock, among which the Holy Spirit has made you overseers, to shepherd the church of God which He purchased with His own blood.
—Acts 20:28 (NKJV)

Our sins have been completely and eternally forgiven by the precious blood of Christ. His blood forgives us.

... in whom we have redemption through His blood, the forgiveness of sins.
—Colossians 1:14 (NKJV)

Justification before God, salvation from judgment and eternal security are given through Jesus's blood. Both our past and future sins have been forgiven. His blood justifies us.

Much more then, having now been justified by His blood, we shall be saved from wrath through Him.
—Romans 5:9 (NKJV)

The authority and dominion of sin has been removed in our lives because of the blood of Jesus. His blood washes us.

... and from Jesus Christ, the faithful witness, the firstborn from the dead, and the ruler over the kings of the earth. To Him who loved us and washed us from our sins in His own blood, which surpasses all understanding is given to us only through the blood His cross.
—Revelation 1:5 (NKJV)

The blood of Jesus is what sets us apart as God's purchased possessions. His blood sanctifies us.

Therefore Jesus also, that He might sanctify the people with His own blood, suffered outside the gate.
—Hebrews 13:12 (NKJV)

Because of the blood of Beautiful Jesus, we can walk in God's light. His blood cleanses us.

But if we walk in the light as He is in the light, we have fellowship with one another, and the blood of Jesus Christ His Son cleanses us from all sin.
—1 John 1:7 (NKJV)

True peace, which encompasses the totality of our lives, only comes through the shed blood of His cross. His blood gives us peace.

... and by Him to reconcile all things to Himself, by Him, whether things on earth or things in heaven, having made peace through the blood of His cross.
—*Colossians 1:20 (NKJV)*

The blood of Jesus imparts boldness into our hearts to approach the throne of God.

Therefore, brethren, having boldness to enter the Holiest by the blood of Jesus ...
—*Hebrews 10:19 (NKJV)*

The beautiful blood of Jesus has a voice that speaks loudly from Heaven. His blood shouts grace, forgiveness, redemption, peace, and healing over us!

... to Jesus the Mediator of the new covenant, and to the blood of sprinkling that speaks better things than that of Abel.
—*Hebrews 12:24 (NKJV)*

Scripture tells us the Satanic kingdom can only be defeated by the spotless blood of the Lamb.

And they overcame him by the blood of the Lamb and by the word of their testimony, and they did not love their lives to the death.
—*Revelation 12:11 (NKJV)*

The blood of Jesus brings us into perfect union and intimacy with Him.

"He who eats My flesh and drinks My blood abides in Me, and I in him."
—John 5:56 (NKJV)

Purposeful Adoration: His Beautiful Blood

Beautiful Jesus, I adore Your holy blood, which has washed away all my sins. Your precious blood has purchased me and set my life apart as Your own special possession. Lord, I will honor and eternally praise the cleansing power of Your beautiful blood.

CHAPTER 15

HIS BEAUTIFUL SCARS

One of the twelve disciples, Thomas (nicknamed the Twin), was not with the others when Jesus came. They told him, "We have seen the Lord!" But he replied, "I won't believe it unless I see the nail wounds in his hands, put my fingers into them, and place my hand into the wound in his side." Eight days later the disciples were together again, and this time Thomas was with them. The doors were locked; but suddenly, as before, Jesus was standing among them. "Peace be with you," he said. Then he said to Thomas, "Put your finger here, and look at my hands. Put your hand into the wound in my side. Don't be faithless any longer. Believe!" "My Lord and my God!" Thomas exclaimed. Then Jesus told him, "You believe because you have seen me. Blessed are those who believe without seeing me."
—John 20:24-29 (NLT)

Visualize the story you just read. Put yourself there. Imagine seeing the beautiful Lord crucified like a criminal. What did it feel like to walk so closely with Him and then see Him die? What heaviness must have been upon the shoulders of the disciples!

Sure, they heard the Lord speak of resurrection, but would there be no room in their minds for doubt? How many times had the Lord grown frustrated with them because of their unbelief? They doubted the possibility of lesser things. Surely they began to doubt their Lord would rise from the dead.

You and I have doubted the Lord in lesser matters. It would be dishonest to claim we have perfect faith all the time. Think of the matters that cause our faith to waver. Now imagine that Jesus, Himself being the source of the miracles they witnessed, is taken away. After the second day of not hearing from Him, knowing He is in a tomb, I can assure you that you would have to fight some level of doubt.

So there they were. The disciples knew their Teacher was in the tomb.

And then they saw Him appear.

Thomas, of course, was not among the first to see the resurrected Lord. He wanted proof. He wanted to touch the scars of Jesus and witness, with his own physical eyes, the living Christ. In Thomas's moment of doubt, Jesus appeared before him. Thomas was able to touch the scars for himself. His response was one of faith, worship, and joy!

"My Lord and my God!"
—John 20:28 (NKJV)

When we come into contact with the nail scars of Jesus, doubt is dispelled and faith is energized. We approach the glorified Lord to worship His nail scars by faith, believing as we practice purposeful adoration. Even if you're like Thomas, and you have seeds of doubt within your heart, you can still act in faith to adore the scars of Jesus. And when you do, doubt will be replaced with soaring faith.

If only you believe, you can come into contact with the body of the Lord by faith through the Spirit.

As we saw with the disciples, the scars of Jesus produce three powerful results in us. Worshipping His nail scars causes us to be:

• Full of faith;
• joyful; and
• fearless.

When you, by means of purposeful adoration, come into contact with the scars of Jesus, faith will replace your doubt. Jesus challenged Thomas's doubt by instructing him to place his hands on the scars. When we need a boost in faith, we can look to the scars of Jesus and catch a glimpse of His identity, power, and victory.

His scars of suffering also produce joy in your life. They produce joy because they are proof of Jesus's victory over all things, including death. His scars represent the price He paid to give you His joy.

Those precious marks also make you fearless. When you know the One Who bears the scars of ultimate victory over death, you are made fearless. After all, if the One Who bears the scars is for you, who can be against you? Even death will lose its power over your life.

TOUCH AND RECEIVE

But we have to touch, in the spirit, the nail scars of Jesus if we are to receive from them. While looking at His beautiful features, we must not forget the scars that mark them.

Jesus is still beckoning you and I to touch, through faith, His nail scars in the act of purposeful adoration. Just as He did for Thomas, the Holy Spirit wants to connect your worship and adoration to the glorified nail scars of the Lord and give you a personal revelation of Jesus.

When we worship the nail scars of Jesus, we receive all they offer. And they offer much! Speaking of Jesus, the Book of Revelation describes how He prevails.

And one of the elders said unto me, "Weep not: behold, the lion of the tribe of Judah, the Root of David, hath prevailed to open the book, and to loose the seven seals."
—Revelation 5:5 (KJV)

The scars of Jesus are the marks of war, and He has prevailed as the victorious King. His scars prove that. They are the divine receipts of His victorious conquest.

Think about this: The heavenly elders focus on the Lord's beautiful nail scars and His blood applied to the mercy seat. When they say He has prevailed, they are saying He has conquered.

He is victorious over all His foes. When you worship through His nail scars, you can see the victorious King who has subdued, overcome, and prevailed against all His enemies on your behalf.

When we focus on the beautiful nail scars of Jesus through purposeful adoration, we can see the glorified and victorious King. Jesus has the proof of victory through His nail scars. He is the mighty Warrior of Heaven.

Saying with a loud voice, Worthy is the Lamb that was slain to receive power, and riches, and wisdom, and strength, and honor, and glory and blessing.
—Revelation 5:12 (KJV)

Because Jesus was slain and rose from the dead, because of His scars, He is worthy to receive:

• Power;
• riches;
• wisdom;
• strength;
• honor;
• glory; and
• blessing.

Jesus not only has received power, but He is our power. He not only received riches; He is our riches. He is our wisdom, strength, honor, glory, and blessing.

Not only did Beautiful Jesus achieve and receive these wellsprings from the Father, but it has become His mission to distribute them. He distributes them through His scars to His people. The scars of Beautiful Jesus are the wellspring of these manifestations.

They looked at His scars—at the proof His conquest—and declared all He was worthy to receive. The scars are what brought those things to Jesus, and the scars are what bring those things through Jesus to us. The purposeful adoration of His scars bring about the same manifestations in your life.

POWER

Beautiful Jesus is your Power.

These words spake Jesus, and lifted up his eyes to heaven, and said, Father, the hour is come; glorify thy Son, that thy Son also may glorify thee: As thou hast given him power over all flesh, that he should give eternal life to as many as thou hast given him.
—John 17:1-2 (KJV)

And declared to be the Son of God with power, according to the spirit of holiness, by the resurrection from the dead.
—Romans 1:4 (KJV)

Jesus is the source of God's power. He is the One Who baptizes us with the Holy Spirit.

*I baptize with water those who repent of their sins and turn to God. But
someone is coming soon who is greater than I am—so much greater that
I'm not worthy even to be his slave and carry his sandals. He will baptize
you with the Holy Spirit and with fire.*
—*Matthew 3:11 (NLT)*

He breathes upon us the power of the Holy Spirit. He enables us to carry
out all His commands and desires.

Then he breathed on them and said, "Receive the Holy Spirit."
—*John 20:22 (NLT)*

It's quite simple, really: When we purposefully adore the scars marking
the beautiful body of the Lord, we receive ultimate power of all sorts.

*But as many as received Him, to them gave He power to become the sons
of God, even to them that believe in His name.*
—*John 1:12 (KJV)*

*And when he had called unto him his twelve disciples, he gave them power
against unclean spirits, to cast them out, and to heal all manner of sickness
and all manner of disease.*
—*Matthew 10:1 (KJV)*

This power continues to flow from His scars well into the day of His
glorious return.

And then shall appear the sign of the Son of man in heaven: and then shall all the tribes of the earth mourn, and they shall see the Son of man coming in the clouds of heaven with power and great glory.
—Matthew 24:30 (KJV)

RICHES

Beautiful Jesus is your riches.

In Genesis 14:21-24, Abram refuses the spoils of the king of Sodom. Though it was an exceedingly great financial reward, Abram did not accept it. It is in this same context that God tells Abram, "I am … thy exceeding great reward."

After these things the word of the Lord came unto Abram in a vision, saying, Fear not, Abram: I am thy shield, and thy exceeding great reward.
—Genesis 15:1 (KJV)

When you purposefully adore His scars, you receive the ultimate riches—Jesus Himself. He is your riches!

The Lord enriches your soul, your body, your finances, and your generations.

And this same God who takes care of me will supply all your needs from his glorious riches, which have been given to us in Christ Jesus.
—Philippians 4:19 (NLT)

But thou shalt remember the LORD thy God: for it is he that giveth thee power to get wealth, that he may establish his covenant which he sware unto thy fathers, as it is this day.
—Deuteronomy 8:18 (KJV)

Wisdom and knowledge is granted unto thee; and I will give thee riches, and wealth, and honour, such as none of the kings have had that have been before thee, neither shall there any after thee have the like.
—2 Chronicles 1:12 (KJV)

WISDOM

Beautiful Jesus is your wisdom.

From His scars also flow the wisdom of the Heavenly Father. Imagine that! The very wisdom which framed the world is available to you because of the victorious scars of Christ.

But of Him are ye in Christ Jesus, who of God is made unto us wisdom, and righteousness, and sanctification and redemption.
—1 Corinthians 1:30 (KJV)

In whom are hid all the treasures of wisdom and knowledge.
—Colossians 2:3 (KJV)

If ever you face a situation in which you find yourself confused, just calm your heart and begin to adore His scars. From them will flow the wisdom of God Himself.

STRENGTH

Beautiful Jesus is your strength.

I will love thee, O Lord, my strength.
—Psalm 18:2 (KJV)

The Lord is my strength and my shield: my heart trusted in Him and I
am helped: therefore my heart greatly rejoiceth; and with my song I will
praise Him.
—Psalm 28:7 (KJV)

A final word: Be strong in the Lord and in his mighty power.
—Ephesians 6:10 (NLT)

When you are weak, when you feel like giving up, look upon His marks
of suffering. He endured much to be your strength. Think of all He had
to endure. The same strength that enabled Jesus to complete His task of
suffering is the same strength that will carry you through whatever you are
facing today.

Touch His scars in faith, and let Him be your strength.

HONOR

Beautiful Jesus is your honor.

Honour and majesty are before him: strength and beauty are in his sanctuary.
—Psalm 96:6 (KJV)

Glory and honour are in his presence; strength and gladness are in his place.
—1 Chronicles 16:27 (KJV)

Both riches and honour come of thee, and thou reignest over all; and in thine hand is power and might; and in thine hand it is to make great, and to give strength unto all.
—1 Chronicles 29:12 (KJV)

Jesus was shamed so He could give you honor. Jesus was humiliated so He could restore your dignity. The degrading power of sin was broken over you because of the humility of Jesus. And now that honor, in which Christ is forever clothed, becomes yours by association. It is simply an honor to be associated with Jesus.

Let the shame of your past be forever erased. Touch the scars, and say goodbye to your shame.

GLORY

Beautiful Jesus is your glory.

But thou, O LORD, art a shield for me, MY GLORY, and the lifter of my head.
—Psalm 3:3 (KJV)

Jesus wants to reveal and impart His glory into every area of your life.

And the glory which You gave Me, I have given to them, that they may be one just as We are one.
—John 17:22 (KJV)

The luminous glory of God is only found in the face of Jesus Christ.

For God, who commanded the light to shine out of darkness, hath shined in our hearts, to give the light of the knowledge of the glory of God in the face of Jesus Christ.
—2 Corinthians 4:6 (KJV)

Jesus is the King of glory. His glory brings strength, might, and protection into your life so you can win every battle you face.

Who is the King of glory? The Lord strong and mighty, the Lord mighty in battle.
—Psalm 24:8 (KJV)

Beautiful Jesus is the Lord of glory.

My brethren, have not the faith of our Lord Jesus Christ, the Lord of glory, with respect of persons.
—James 2:1 (KJV)

The glory of the Father belongs to Jesus. When beautiful Jesus surrounds you with His glory, the angels will constantly dwell around you. That same glory will appear with Jesus at His return.

For the Son of Man will come with his angels in the glory of his Father and will judge all people according to their deeds.
—Matthew 16:27 (NLT)

The manifestation of the glory of Jesus will cause an atmosphere of signs and wonders to erupt all around you.

This beginning of miracles did Jesus in Cana of Galilee, and manifested forth his glory; and his disciples believed on him.
—John 2:11 (KJV)

BLESSING

Beautiful Jesus is your blessing. He was also Abraham's seed of blessing.

And in thy seed shall all the nations of the earth be blessed; because thou hast obeyed My voice.
—Genesis 22:18 (KJV)

He Himself is blessed.

Blessed be the God and Father of our Lord Jesus Christ, who hath blessed us with all spiritual blessings in heavenly places in Christ.
—Ephesians 1:3 (KJV)

Saying, Blessed be the King that cometh in the name of the Lord: peace in heaven, and glory in the highest.
—Luke 19:38 (KJV)

Blessed art thou, O LORD: teach me thy statutes.
—Psalm 119:12 (KJV)

We receive all that is His when we bless His name. When we bless His name, He blesses our lives. When we bless Him with our praise and thank Him for the scars He bears, we receive His blessing.

The Lamb Who Was Slain

Imagine Jesus holding up His nail-scarred hands in a demonstration of total victory. He completed the conquest to become the glorified, beautiful Jesus, and the elders bow down on their faces before Him. Indeed, worthy is the Lamb Who was slain.

But I want you not just to receive the benefits of His scars. I want you to come to a better understanding of the sacrifice of the scars themselves.

Appreciating what He did is simple: Just meditate upon His beautiful features, and then imagine His features being broken for you.

This is what the Scripture says about the suffering of Beautiful Jesus.

For he shall grow up before him as a tender plant, and as a root out of a dry ground: he hath no form nor comeliness; and when we shall see him, there is no beauty that we should desire him.
—Isaiah 53:2 (KJV)

His eyes—His beautiful eyes of love—were blindfolded so we could see God. His arms, which embraced the little children, were tied to the cross.

His beautiful hands, which bring healing, were nailed. They were pierced so we could handle the power of the Holy Spirit through our hands. His feet that walked on water were nailed to the cross so we could walk with God.

His mouth, which spoke the eternal word of life, tasted bitterness and death so we could taste His goodness. That same mouth was kept closed as Jesus was accused. Through it, Jesus uttered not a word while sinful men spoke evil of Him. As a lamb is led in silence to the slaughter, so Jesus opened not His mouth. His forehead bore a crown of thorns so we could wear a crown of gold. He wore a crown of thorns so we could wear a crown of life. His bare, bleeding back was scraped by the wooden cross so we could sit on thrones in glory. His almighty ears, which heard the Father's voice speaking audibly, heard the mockery of His accusers while He hung on the cross.

His body was stripped naked and beaten so we could be clothed with His righteousness. He was humiliated so we could wear robes of righteousness and be exalted. He was covered in spittle so we could be covered in the anointing. He was ridiculed at the cross so we could find our identity.

Picture what Jesus endured, as His physical features began to bear the weight of our sin. His body took the curse and power of sin upon itself. God allowed Jesus to become our sin offering.

For He hath made Him to be sin for us; who knew no sin, so that we might be made the righteousness of God in Him.
—2 Corinthians 5:1 (KJV)

The condemnation and guilt of our sin, like leprosy, rested upon His beautiful features. Our sin was transferred onto the spotless Lamb, and His righteousness was transferred onto us.

His lovely hands felt the sensation of practicing wickedness. His beautiful feet bore the guilt of walking the path of the unrighteous. His mind fought our thoughts of covetousness and misdoing. Imagine the moment-by-moment battle the perfect Son of God endured. By becoming our sin offering, Jesus, the Word of God Himself, experienced the horror and punishment of sin. Jesus became intimately familiar with what God never knew, and He conquered it victoriously for you.

So focus on the worth of the Lamb that was slain when you practice purposefully adoring His marks. This activates His manifestations—that is, the manifestations of power, riches, wisdom, strength, honor, glory, and blessing.

PURPOSEFUL ADORATION:
HIS BEAUTIFUL SCARS

Beautiful Jesus, I am in awe of all You accomplished and amazed by Your victory. I worship Your beautiful scars, Your symbols of victorious conquest. Because of Your scars, I am full of faith, joyful, and fearless. I reach out now in faith and touch Your scars. And from them, I receive power, riches, wisdom, strength, honor, glory, and blessings. Thank You, Jesus, for choosing to receive Your beautiful scars. Amen.

CHAPTER 15

BEAUTIFUL JESUS IN YOU

As you begin to practice the art of purposeful adoration, you will, of course, receive the many benefits and experiences I described in this book. But no experience or benefit is as rewarding as what reaching the pinnacle of purposeful adoration will cause. Ultimately, the reward and primary effect of purposeful adoration is simply this: oneness.

That's all we desire, isn't it?

Oneness with Jesus …

… because as He is, so are we in this world.
—1 John 4:17 (KJV)

I can't shake that timeless truth from my mind. Those words stay with me constantly. As He is, so am I in this world. As He is, so are you in this world. Think about that: As His eyes are, so are mine. As His ears are, so are mine. As His mouth is, so is mine. And so on.

As you worship the Lord, as you adore His every feature, you begin to exchange self for Christ. You even begin to exchange consciousness. Something beautiful happens in you as you adore beautiful Jesus: You put on Christ.

But put ye on the Lord Jesus Christ, and make not provision for the flesh, to fulfil the lusts thereof.
—Romans 13:14 (KJV)

You see, as you continue along in the lifestyle of purposeful adoration, eventually, something beautiful begins to happen. You begin to become one with the Lord. This means you begin to decrease, and He begins to increase. You look more and more like Jesus every moment.

While the purposeful adoration of every feature of Christ can cause oneness to transpire, there is one feature of the Lord that is special: The scar from the spear that pierced His side.

THE SPEAR SCAR

But whosoever drinketh of the water that I shall give him shall never thirst; but the water that I shall give him shall be in him a well of water springing up into everlasting life.
—John 4:14 (KJV)

What is this water of which Jesus speaks? The water Jesus gives us represents His life force, His Holy Spirit, and His indwelling Presence.

That holy presence, that living water, becomes a well in you—a fountain or a spring gushing upward from deep within your soul into the glorified Lord. This well within us is the Spirit of Christ Himself Who carries our love, our thoughts, our prayers, and even our consciousness.

When waters merge, it is impossible to tell them apart. The same is true of your being and the Lord's being. In the spirit, there is a deep mingling of your spirit and the Holy Spirit.

So from where did this living water first flow? It first flowed at the cross, as the blood and water poured out of His side, when He was pierced with a spear!

One of the soldiers, however, pierced his side with a spear, and immediately blood and water flowed out.
—John 19:34 (NLT)

That same living water then flowed into our soul, creating a fountain of water in us. And the cycle continues, for that same water in us then flows upward back into Christ Jesus. This connects us with Him eternally.

Let me explain it to you this way: Living water flowed from Jesus at the cross. The very same flows from within us. That water then flows "up into everlasting life." Do you see the cycle? Can you see the merging of your inner man with Christ's Holy Spirit? As these waters begin to mingle, they become impossible to separate or distinguish from one another.

Jesus said He would put a fountain within us that would be springing, gushing, and flowing upward into everlasting life. So His Holy Spirit makes us one with the inner being of Jesus.

However, before the Holy Spirit came at Pentecost, before living water began to flow out of the members of the early Church, His beautiful side gushed with water. The spear scar of Jesus is, therefore, the door into His wonderful soul, which is our holy of holies. The spear scar is the point of oneness with the Lord.

Beautiful Jesus is the secret place of the Most High, and His beautiful spear scar is the entrance into the secret place.

The fountain of the Water of Life flows directly from Jesus Himself.

And he said unto me, It is done. I am Alpha and Omega, the beginning and the end. I will give unto him that is athirst of the fountain of the water of life freely.
—Revelation 21:6 (KJV)

The pure river of the water of life flows from Jesus to us, and from us to Jesus. It's a beautiful cycle of oneness that draws us closer and closer to the Lord as the waters make their movements. In fact, I believe the river of life is a two-way stream: We are flowing to Jesus in a stream every time we practice purposeful adoration, and the Lord is flowing back to us. He flows into us, and we flow back into Him.

And he shewed me a pure river of water of life, clear as crystal, proceeding out of the throne of God and of the Lamb.
—Revelation 22:1 (KJV)

The origin and destination of the living water of God is the beautiful spear scar of Jesus. Enter into that door today.

ONENESS

Oneness is the pinnacle of purposeful adoration. Every prayer, every song, every breath whispered in adoration for the features of Christ will bring you closer to the Lord and make you more like Him. Purposeful adoration will cause your ears, eyes, hands, legs, mouth, and being to become His.

It is through worshipping Him that we become more like Him. It is in surrendering to Him that we become most like Him. It is through taking our time to appreciate the power of His every feature that we receive the most from Him.

Reach out now. Touch the spear scar. Let the Holy Spirit stir within your heart a deep passion for each and every attribute of Beautiful Jesus. Just look at Him, and let worship overtake your heart. Then let that worship cause you to be no more—leaving room for the features of Jesus to take the place of yours. Simply behold Him and be transformed. Become one with the resurrected, glorified Lord.

So all of us who have had that veil removed can see and reflect the glory of the Lord. And the Lord—who is the Spirit—makes us more and more like him as we are changed into his glorious image.
—2 Corinthians 3:18 (NLT)

Let the beauty of the Lord shine through you. May your very body begin to emanate with the glory of God, as you surrender your being through the intimate prayers of purposeful adoration. With your heart full of faith, pray this beautiful prayer now:

Beautiful Jesus,
Thank You for revealing to me the power of Your every attribute.
Help me to never again overlook the divine beauty to be found in Your
features.
I want You to overtake me. When others look at me, let them see through
me, right into You. Thank You for the holy privilege of oneness with Your
beautiful being.
Beautiful Jesus, let Your heavenly gaze rest upon my countenance.
Beautiful Jesus, be beautiful in me.